OUR GREAT SALVATION

OUR GREAT SALVATION
And Other Sermons

by
Oliver B. Greene

The Gospel Hour, Inc., Oliver B. Greene, Director
P. O. Box 2024, Greenville, South Carolina

CONTENTS

OUR GREAT SALVATION

OUR GREAT SALVATION

"Therefore we ought to give the more earnest heed to the things which we have heard, lest at any time we should let them slip. For if the word spoken by angels was stedfast, and every transgression and disobedience received a just recompence of reward; how shall we escape, if we neglect so great salvation; which at the first began to be spoken by the Lord, and was confirmed unto us by them that heard Him; God also bearing them witness, both with signs and wonders, and with divers miracles, and gifts of the Holy Ghost, according to His own will?" (Heb. 2:1–4).

The text: *"How shall we escape, if we neglect so great salvation?"*

This "great salvation" about which we are to study in this message is great in *three ways*:

Our Salvation Is Great in Its COST

I am wondering if someone is not saying, "Mr. Greene, have not I heard you and many other preachers make the statement that all one need do to be saved is to receive the finished work of Jesus? Have you not many times said on the radio, 'Bow your head, confess your sins, call on the name of Jesus—and He will save you'?"

I am guilty — I plead guilty to that charge; and if Jesus lets me live and He tarries, you will hear me say that ten thousand times more—on the radio, in the tent meetings, in churches, and in my printed sermons. All any poor sinner can do to be saved is to *receive the finished work of the Lord Jesus*. Salvation is a *gift*, and "Whosoever shall call upon the name of the Lord shall be saved!" (Rom. 10:13).

9

Perhaps someone is saying, "What is great about *that*?" Dear friend, it cost God the brightest Jewel in heaven to make possible our salvation: "God so loved the world, that *He gave His only begotten Son*, that whosoever believeth in Him should not perish, but have everlasting life" (John 3:16).

God loved us while we were yet unlovely. God gave His Son to die for His enemies: "For scarcely for a righteous man will one die: yet peradventure for a good man some would even dare to die. But God commendeth His love toward us, in that, while we were yet sinners, Christ died for us" (Rom. 5:7,8).

I repeat: It cost God His only begotten Son to make possible our salvation.

It cost *heaven* the most precious Jewel there. Surely the angels must have bowed their heads. Surely the cherubim must have folded their wings; surely heaven went into mourning when it was announced that the Son, the Pearl of Great Price, would leave heaven's glory and in one gigantic step would come to earth's sorrow to lay His life down for sinners!

That leads me to say that it not only cost *God* His only Son, and cost *heaven* the most precious Jewel there, but it cost the *Son* every drop of His precious blood to make possible our salvation. Every pain He suffered—soul, spirit, and body—every tear He shed, every heartache He endured, every miracle He performed, every good deed He did, every step He walked on this earth, every lash they put on His back, the crown of thorns He wore on His head, the scourging, the mocking, the spittle in His face, the plucking off of the hair from His cheeks, the spikes in His feet, the terrible cry of agony—"My God, My God, why hast Thou forsaken Me?" — all these things were

10

necessary that we might be able to call upon the name of the Lord and be saved.

If Jesus had not prayed, "Father, if it be possible let this cup pass from Me — nevertheless, not as I will, but as Thou wilt," He could never have said, "It is finished." And if He had never said, "It is finished," we could have never called upon His name and found salvation. So let me hasten to say that the most expensive thing in heaven or earth or under the earth, the most expensive thing known to God or the angels (or to all creation), the most valuable thing ever known is *our salvation*.

We are purchased at the tremendous price of the shed blood of Jesus Christ. We are *redeemed* through the *power* of His shed blood. We are *kept* because He suffered, died, was buried, and rose again. Because He lives, *we* live. Because He conquered, *we* conquer. Because He paid the debt, *we go free.* In Jesus Christ there is redemption: "But of Him are ye in Christ Jesus, who of God is made unto us wisdom, and righteousness, and sanctification, and redemption: That, according as it is written, He that glorieth, let Him glory in the Lord" (I Cor. 1:30,31).

Christ is made unto us *wisdom* — the wisdom through which we call. Christ is made unto us *righteousness*; He who knew no sin was made sin for us, that we in Him might become righteous (II Cor. 5:21). Christ is made unto us *sanctification*; He sanctified Himself that we might be sanctified. Christ is made unto us *redemption*; everything that Adam lost, Jesus redeemed at the tremendous price of His precious blood. Through His blood we have redemption, the forgiveness of sins — and without the shedding of blood there is no remission. The blood of Jesus Christ, God's Son, cleanseth us from all sin! Let me repeat for emphasis: The most precious, priceless thing

11

known to God or man is salvation.

Yes, this salvation is *great* in its *cost*.

The only possible way poor, miserable, wretched, despicable sinners could have been transformed into heirs of God, joint-heirs with Christ (we are sons of God), is through God's great love. We were, in times past, children of wrath. We walked according to this world, according to the prince of the power of the air, who is the devil. We had our conversation, in times past, in the lust of our flesh. We fulfilled the desires of the mind and of the flesh, and we were by nature the children of wrath. "BUT GOD, WHO IS RICH IN MERCY, FOR HIS GREAT LOVE WHEREWITH HE LOVED US, even when we were dead in sins, hath quickened us together with Christ, (by grace ye are saved)" (Eph. 2:4,5). We have salvation because God loved us with a "GREAT LOVE." God's love is a fathomless ocean . . . a mine of wealth. His love is a lasting spring, an artesian well, a glorious provision, a sun of warmth, a gigantic lifting power. His love is an unceasing inspiration! No wonder the Holy Ghost refers to the love that saved us as "GREAT LOVE."

Those of us who are saved are saved with a *"great salvation"*—great because God is its source; great because we are salvation's object . . . enemies of God when God provided this great salvation. *Christ IS this salvation.* Deliverance from sin, the devil, and hell is the *meaning* of our great salvation. It is powerful to deliver us from the world, the flesh, and the devil. Faith receives this great salvation; holiness in Christ is the result, and glory in heaven with Jesus is its consummation. Yes, our salvation is truly GREAT.

Those of us who possess this great salvation are thrilled with great joy that is unspeakable and full of glory.

12

In the book of Acts, Philip went down to Samaria and preached the Gospel of the Lord Jesus Christ. Many were born again, brought into the knowledge of this great salvation, and the Bible tells us, "There was GREAT JOY in that city" (Acts 8:8).

When the angel announced the birth of Jesus, he said, "Fear not: for, behold, I bring you good tidings of GREAT JOY, which shall be to all people" (Luke 2:10). The *Saviour* is the *secret* of the joy of this great salvation. He is not only the secret—He is the *substance* of it. He is the *supply*. He is the *source*. He *is* this "great salvation." HIS joy makes *our* joy full and lasting. I especially love the way Peter expresses the joy of our salvation: "Whom having not seen, ye love; in whom, though now ye see Him not, yet believing, ye rejoice with JOY UNSPEAKABLE AND FULL OF GLORY" (I Pet. 1:8).

Those of us who possess this great salvation are strengthened with great power: "And with GREAT POWER gave the apostles witness of the resurrection of the Lord Jesus: and great grace was upon them all" (Acts 4:33). From any angle you may look at this great salvation, from whatever aspect we study this great salvation, we find that it is GREAT!

Our great salvation brings to our heart *great peace*: "GREAT PEACE have they which love thy law: and nothing shall offend them" (Psa. 119:165). To love God's holy Word is to find the joy of His great grace and salvation, the tenderness of His love, the holiness of Himself, and the peace that passeth all understanding. To the disciples Jesus said, "Peace I leave with you, my peace I give unto you: not as the world giveth, give I unto you. Let not your heart be troubled, neither let it be afraid" (John 14:27). This *great salvation* brings *great PEACE*

13

to our hearts.

One of these glorious days when Jesus comes to the world, His saints will come with Him. He will come first in the *Rapture* FOR them—and then when He returns to the earth, we (the Bride) will return *with* Him. He will come in *great glory*: "And then shall they see the Son of man coming in a cloud with power and *great glory*"(Luke 21:27). He will not have that glory apart from His saints—His Bride. It would be no glory to Him if we were not with Him, because He *purchased* us . . . He purchased the Church with His own precious blood.

God's *mercy* is so great that He forgives great sins committed by great sinners over a great period of time; and then He gives great favor and blessing and great privileges to these great sinners who are recipients of His great mercy. He gives to us great pleasures in this life and eternal enjoyment in the great heaven of the great God. The only kind of mercy, grace, and love God knows is GREAT; therefore, "How shall we escape, if we neglect so great salvation?"

Hear these words: "Whosoever shall call upon the name of the Lord shall be saved." Jesus said, "Come unto me, all ye that labour and are heavy laden, and I will give you rest," and "Him that cometh to me I will in no wise cast out." These are precious words: "As many as received Him, to them gave He power to become the sons of God, even to them that believe on His name: Which were born . . . of God."

These words are not to be taken lightly: "Believe on the Lord Jesus Christ, and thou shalt be saved." Yes, salvation has been brought down. Salvation is *finished.* Salvation is presented to you, dear reader, and the only way you or I or any other person will ever be saved is to

14

simply receive the finished work of the Lord Jesus by faith . . . trust Him, believe on Him—and HE does the saving! How shall we escape if we neglect salvation that *cost so much* and has been made so plain?

Our Salvation Is Great in Its SCOPE

"For God so loved THE WORLD, that He gave His only begotten Son, that whosoever believeth in Him should not perish, but have everlasting life" (John 3:16). This verse has been called "the Gospel in a nutshell"—and truly it is. There are *two things* I would like to point out here:

1. *God loved the world* — the whole world, all the world, every human being who has ever set foot on this earth. God loved ALL.

2. *"Whosoever believeth"* on Jesus shall be saved—shall have everlasting life. John 3:16 does not teach that a select, elect, predestined group can be saved, and all others must be damned. John 3:16 teaches clearly that God loved the *world*, Jesus died for the *world*, and *whosoever will* can be saved.

There are those who teach that only a selected group known as "the elect" will be saved. I believe in the sovereignty of God. God knows who *will* be saved and who will *not* be saved. God is omnipotent, omniscient, and omnipresent — but the fact that God is sovereign does not determine whether I spend eternity in heaven or in hell.

"He that believeth on Him is not condemned: but he that believeth not is condemned already, because he hath not believed in the name of the only begotten Son of God" (John 3:18). In this verse we are clearly taught that *believers* are *free from condemnation*. *Unbelievers* are *condemned*. The reason? Because they *believe not* on the

15

name of the Son of God.

If the doctrine of hyper-Calvinism is true, then why did not the Holy Spirit clearly say, "He that believeth not is condemned already *because he was not elected*"? It is left up to the *individual* to decide whether to *believe* or to *refuse* to believe on the Lord Jesus Christ unto salvation. The SCOPE of our great salvation takes in *everyone*, excludes *no one*. Regardless of your nationality, the color of your skin, your social standing, your political standing, your monetary standing . . . *"whosoever will"* can be saved.

"The Lord is not slack concerning His promise, as some men count slackness; but is longsuffering to us-ward, *not willing* that *any* should perish, but that ALL should come to repentance" (II Pet. 3:9).

The Lord is not willing that any should perish, but that all (*everyone*) should come to repentance. God has no joy in the death of the wicked. Let me say without apology and without reservation, if you die in your sins and wake up in hell-fire, it will not be because you were not "elected" or "predestined" or "chosen"; it will not be the will of God. *It will be because of your own stubborn will and your refusal to believe on the Lord Jesus Christ as your personal Saviour.*

When Jesus came to this earth, the earth was filled with "religion" — the scribes and the Pharisees, the elders and the chief priests; and at that particular time God was dealing with a specific nation — Israel. The Gentiles and all others were "dogs" in the eyes of the Israelites . . . they were outcasts, aliens, without hope, and strangers to the covenant of promise (Eph. 2:12). How refreshing it must have been to the ears of the poor lepers, the downcast, the outcast, when Jesus said, "Come unto me, ALL

16

YE THAT LABOUR AND ARE HEAVY LADEN, and I will give you rest!" (Matt. 11:28).

If the doctrine of hyper-Calvinism is true—if there are chosen ones who can be saved and all others must be damned—then why did not Jesus say, "Come unto me, *all the elect*, and I will give you rest"? Why did He not invite, "Come unto me, all the *chosen*—and I will give you rest"? Why did He not say, "Come unto me, all ye *predestined*—and I will give you rest"? Do you know why He did not say that? Jesus came into the world to save *"whosoever"* from *whatsoever* sin was damning them. Jesus came to save the Jew, the Gentile, the rich, the poor, the bond, the free, the down and out, the up and out — *"whosoever"* was His invitation. ALL are invited to come, and *whosoever comes* can be saved.

The Apostle Paul declares: "That if thou shalt confess with thy mouth the Lord Jesus, and shalt believe in thine heart that God hath raised Him from the dead, thou shalt be saved. For with the heart man believeth unto righteousness; and with the mouth confession is made unto salvation. For the Scripture saith, Whosoever believeth on Him shall not be ashamed. For there is no difference between the Jew and the Greek: for the same Lord over all is rich unto *all* that call upon Him. For *WHOSOEVER SHALL CALL upon the name of the Lord SHALL BE SAVED"* (Rom. 10:9—13). Thank God, the invitation is to all . . . ALL are included, NOT ONE is excluded.

Hear the last invitation to sinners given in the Bible: "And the Spirit and the bride say, Come. And let him that heareth say, Come. And let him that is athirst come. And WHOSOEVER WILL, *let him take the water of life* FREELY" (Rev. 22:17). The Holy Spirit invites ALL to come. The Church (the Bride) invites ALL to come. The

17

invitation is to the thirsty. Why did not the Spirit of God say, "Let him that is elected, come"? Or "Let him that is chosen, come"? Simply because the invitation is to *whosoever is thirsty*! If you are hungry and thirsty for God, you are invited to come—regardless of who you are, regardless of what you have done. If you are thirsty for God and for salvation, come to the Lord Jesus and HE will satisfy your thirst. *"Whosoever will*, let him drink of the water of life freely!"

God created man in His own image (Gen. 1:26,27). God breathed into his nostrils the breath of life, and man became a living soul. God put Adam in the Garden of Eden. He gave Adam instructions. Adam, of his own free will, chose to believe and follow his wife's invitation instead of obeying God's command; therefore, Adam fell into sin and death; and through the disobedience of one man, sin and death moved upon all men. But thank God, God so loved man and the whole wide world, that He gave His only begotten Son that *whosoever*—ANY man desiring to be saved—could be saved.

"Wherefore, as by one man sin entered into the world, and death by sin; and so death passed upon all men, for that all have sinned: (For until the law sin was in the world: but sin is not imputed when there is no law. Nevertheless death reigned from Adam to Moses, even over them that had not sinned after the similitude of Adam's transgression, who is the figure of Him that was to come. But not as the offence, so also is the free gift. For if through the offence of one many be dead, much more the grace of God, and the gift by grace, which is by one man, Jesus Christ, hath abounded unto many. And not as it was by one that sinned, so is the gift: for the judgment was by one to condemnation, but the free gift is of many offences unto justification. For if by one man's offence death reigned by one; much more they which receive abundance of grace and of the gift of righteousness shall reign in life by one, Jesus Christ.) Therefore as by the offence of one judgment came upon all men to condemnation; even so by the righteousness of one the free gift came upon all men unto justification of life. For as by one man's disobedience many were made sinners, so by the obedience of one shall many be made righteous. Moreover the law entered, that the offence might abound. But where sin abounded, grace did much more abound: that as sin hath reigned unto death, even so might grace reign through righteousness unto eternal life by Jesus Christ our Lord" (Rom. 5:12—21).

Please read verse 18 very carefully – and believe it: "'Therefore as by the offence of one judgment came upon ALL men to condemnation; even so by the righteousness of one the free gift *came upon ALL MEN* unto justification of life."

Through the sin of Adam, all died spiritually. We are born in sin, shapen in iniquity. But hallelujah! Through the obedience of the second Adam ALL can be saved—all who *desire* to be saved and who come to God by Christ Jesus.

There is a verse in the Old Testament that will stop every mouth that preaches that some are selected, elected, and chosen, while others must be damned: "ALL we like sheep have gone astray; we have turned every one to his own way; and the Lord hath laid on Him the iniquity of us ALL" (Isa. 53:6). Notice carefully: ALL mankind went astray. ALL have sinned and come short of the glory of God. There is NONE righteous, no, not one! We have ALL gone out of the way – but Jehovah God laid on Jesus *the iniquity of us all.* Jesus paid the penalty for every sin that has been committed by every man – from Adam through the last man who will live on this earth in a natural body. Jesus shed enough blood to cover every sin that

19

ever has been committed, that is being committed, or that ever *will be* committed. Jesus died for the sins of the whole wide world — and *"whosoever will"* may drink freely of the water of life and be saved by the marvelous grace of God, and have their name written in the Lamb's book of Life.

John gives us these precious words: "My little children, these things write I unto you, that ye sin not. And if any man sin, we have an advocate with the Father, Jesus Christ the righteous: *and He is the propitiation for OUR sins: and not for our's only, but ALSO FOR THE SINS OF THE WHOLE WORLD"* (I John 2:1,2).

Jesus died according to the Scriptures. He was buried and He rose again according to the Scriptures. He said, "He that heareth my Word, and believeth on Him that sent me, hath everlasting life, and shall not come into condemnation; but is passed from death unto life" (John 5:24). That is God's holy Word, and it cannot be changed or altered in spite of the hyper-Calvinists and those who teach that only a select, elect, chosen group will be saved.

Let me assure you again that I believe in the sovereignty of God — but I also believe in the free will of man. God made man a free moral agent. He has given man the opportunity to *choose* — and your eternal destiny depends upon whether you *receive* or *reject* the Lord Jesus Christ. Receive Him — and live! But if you reject Him, you will spend eternity in the lake of fire that burns with brimstone—not because it is God's will, not because you were not elected to be saved . . . but because of your own stubborn will—because you chose to serve self and sin and lust instead of receiving the Lord Jesus Christ. "Believe on the Lord Jesus Christ, and thou shalt be saved—and thy house" (Acts 16:31).

"How shall we escape, if we neglect so great salvation?" — great *first* in its *cost, second* in its *scope.*

Our Salvation Is Great in Its CLIMAX

"For if we believe that Jesus died and rose again, even so them also which sleep in Jesus will God bring with Him. For this we say unto you by the word of the Lord, that we which are alive and remain unto the coming of the Lord shall not prevent them which are asleep. For the Lord Himself shall descend from heaven with a shout, with the voice of the archangel, and with the trump of God: and the dead in Christ shall rise first: Then we which are alive and remain shall be caught up together with them in the clouds, to meet the Lord in the air: and so shall we ever be with the Lord. WHEREFORE COMFORT ONE ANOTHER WITH THESE WORDS" (I Thess. 4:14–18).

This salvation that we have in the Lord Jesus Christ saves us from the penalty of sin. The wages of sin is death. The *penalty* of sin is death. When sin is finished it brings forth death. Death and sin are synonymous. But when we are saved we are delivered from the power of death. We are raised from spiritual deadness: "And you hath He quickened (made alive), who were dead in trespasses and sins" (Eph. 2:1). Paul declares, "She that liveth in pleasure is dead while she liveth" (I Tim. 5:6). Sin and death are synonymous—but when we are born again we are alive in Christ with a life that is everlasting. We live forever because HE lives forever. We have eternal life because "from everlasting to everlasting, thou art God!" (Psa. 90:1,2).

This salvation saves us from the *penalty* of sin — but that is not all. This great salvation saves us from the *power* of sin. "We are *more than conquerors* through Him that loved us" (Rom. 8:31–39). Read those verses carefully. We overcome the world because greater is the God

21

who is in us than the god of this world—who, of course, is the devil (I John 4:4). *We conquer because God lives in us.* "(Whosoever) is born of God overcometh the world: and this is the victory that overcometh the world, even our faith" (I John 5:4).

This great salvation saves from the *penalty* of sin and daily saves us from the *power* of sin — and then at the end of life's journey it will save us from the very *presence* of sin. If we live until the Rapture of the Church, we believers will be caught up to meet Jesus in the clouds in the air; but if we should depart this life before the Rapture, "to be absent from the body is to be *present with the Lord.*" (Please read II Corinthians 5:1–8.) When a believer dies, he goes immediately to be with the Lord Jesus.

"For to me to live is Christ, and *to die is GAIN.* But if I live in the flesh, this is the fruit of my labour: yet what I shall choose I wot not. For I am in a strait betwixt two, having a desire to depart, and to *be with Christ; which is far better*: nevertheless to abide in the flesh is more needful for you" (Phil. 1:21–24). Paul testified, "To die is gain." He said, "I desire to leave this world and to be with Christ, which would be far better." The salvation we have does not stop or cease at the grave. When we depart this life, we go immediately to be with the Lord Jesus in paradise.

We read in Luke 16 that the rich man died and opened his eyes in hell. The beggar Lazarus died and was carried by the angels into Abraham's bosom—the place of rest, the paradise of the righteous. Thank God for so great salvation!

Not only will this salvation take us to paradise into the presence of the Lord Jesus Christ—but hear these precious words: "Behold, what manner of love the Father hath bestowed upon us, that we should be called the sons of God: therefore the world knoweth us not, because it knew Him not. Beloved, now are we the sons of God, and it doth not yet appear what we shall be: but we know that, when He shall appear, we shall be like Him; for we shall see Him as He is" (I John 3:1,2).

This great salvation provides redemption for the spirit and a body just like the Lord's glorious body for the world to come. We will have a body that will never be sick, never hurt, never die. We will be like Him, we will see Him as He is. I am looking forward to that grand and glorious day when I will have a body untouched by sin — a glorified body like unto His resurrection body.

I am so happy that I can say with David, "The Lord is my Shepherd; I shall not want. He maketh me to lie down in green pastures: He leadeth me beside the still waters. He restoreth my soul: He leadeth me in the paths of righteousness for His name's sake. *Yea, though I walk through the valley of the shadow of death, I WILL FEAR NO EVIL: FOR THOU ART WITH ME; thy rod and thy staff they comfort me.* Thou preparest a table before me in the presence of mine enemies: thou anointest my head with oil; my cup runneth over. Surely goodness and mercy shall follow me all the days of my life: *and I will dwell in the house of the Lord for ever*" (Psalm 23). Hallelujah! The Lord is *my* Shepherd — and if I DO walk through the valley of the shadow of death I will not be afraid, for Jesus will be with me. He will hold my hand. What a great provision in a great salvation!

I know that goodness and mercy will follow me every day that I live on this earth. Then when I depart this life I will dwell in the house of God forever. Jesus said He would go to prepare a place for me and that He would come again and receive me unto Himself (John 14:1–6) — and I am looking forward to that glorious day.

In closing let me give you a precious, precious promise: "And I heard a voice from heaven saying unto me, Write, Blessed are the dead which die in the Lord from henceforth: Yea, saith the Spirit, that they may rest from their labours; and their works do follow them" (Rev. 14:13).

I know I am saved. I am happy in the Lord. It is a great thrill to live for Jesus and try to win others to the Lamb of God. I am glad that my redemption was finished on Calvary. I am redeemed by and through His precious blood. But my salvation did not stop with redemption. I am glad that He gives me the grace, the courage, and the power to LIVE for Him daily. He will not permit me to be tempted above that which I am able to bear, but He will with the temptation make a way for me to escape (I Cor. 10:13). Read it, memorize it, believe it, live by it, and die by it.

What a joy to know that the climax of my salvation will not be at the grave: I will either go to be with Jesus in the Rapture, or if He delays His coming He will go with me through the valley of the shadow, all the way to the paradise of God.

This great salvation brings great joy to my heart because I am redeemed, I know that "He is able to keep that which I have committed unto Him against that day," I know that at the end of life's journey Jesus will be waiting and He will give me a resting place in paradise. In the sweet by-and-by He will give me a body just like His own glorious body, and I will dwell with Him in that celestial city which John saw coming down from God out of heaven, adorned as a bride for her husband.

Do you know this great salvation? If you do not,

24

please bow your head, close your eyes, and receive the Lord Jesus right now! "As many as received Him, to them gave He power to become the sons of God, even to them that believe on His name: which were born . . . of God" (John 1:12,13). Accept this great salvation and then you, too, will be blessed . . . you, too, can say, "Blessed assurance, Jesus is mine! Oh, what a foretaste of glory divine!"

May God bless you richly if you are born again — and may God *save* you, my dear reader, if you are not saved.

CHRIST—HIS RICHES, HIS POVERTY

CHRIST – HIS RICHES, HIS POVERTY

"For ye know the grace of our Lord Jesus Christ, that, though He was rich, yet for your sakes He became poor, that ye through His poverty might be rich" (II Cor. 8:9).

Here is presented one of the most blessed pictures of grace in the entire Bible. To appreciate the grace of our Lord Jesus Christ we must understand His *riches*, we must understand His *poverty*, and then we must see *the riches WE have in HIM.*

We are saved by grace through faith — but I wonder how many of us have ever stopped to reason out just what grace IS and what it cost the Lord Jesus to *provide* saving grace for poor, hell-deserving sinners?

We will never fully understand the grace of God while we dwell in these tabernacles of flesh. One cannot fully appreciate the vastness of the ocean until he has sailed for days without sight of land. When we stand on the beach and look out over the ocean it does not seem so great; but when we start sailing toward the far horizon we realize we have not comprehended its magnitude; there is more than can be seen at one time. We might compare God's grace with the ocean. Our vision is so limited it will take all the ages of eternity for us to realize the fulness of God's marvelous grace!

The Apostle Paul had a wonderful understanding of the grace of God and the exceeding riches of Christ. He said, "Unto me, who am less than the least of all saints, is this grace given, that I should preach among the Gentiles the unsearchable riches of Christ" (Eph. 3:8).

It was Paul who prayed for the removal of the thorn

in his flesh — but he did not argue when God assured him, "My grace is sufficient for thee: for my strength is made perfect in weakness" (II Cor. 12:8,9). He knew that he would be given grace to overcome the thorn even though the Lord did not see fit to remove it.

In Ephesians 1:18,19 Paul speaks of the eyes of our understanding being enlightened, "that ye may know what is the hope of His calling, *and what the riches of the glory of His inheritance in the saints*, and what is the exceeding greatness of His power to us-ward who believe, according to the working of His mighty power."

THE LORD JESUS WAS RICH

1.   He was rich in possessions:

Have you ever really given thought to the riches Christ left when He came into this world? Have you ever really considered the estate He gave up to come into this poverty-stricken universe?

Consider Colossians 1:16,17: *"For by Him were all things created, that are in heaven, and that are in earth, visible and invisible, whether they be thrones, or dominions, or principalities, or powers: all things were created by Him, and for Him: And He is before all things, and by Him all things consist."*

We read of mansions and estates of men, the vast plantations of this earth; but earth holds no estates comparable to that of the Lord Jesus Christ — yet He left it all to die for you and for me! He left His glorious estate and became poor, that WE, *through His poverty*, might be made rich.

The heavens and all of the planets are His — the sun, the moon, the stars were all formed by His hands — but He surrendered them all and took a mortal body, to come to earth and lay down His life for sinners, "that He by the

30

grace of God should taste death for every man'' (Heb. 2:9).

No wonder the Psalmist exclaimed, "Praise ye the Lord! Praise ye the Lord from the heavens: praise Him in the heights. Praise ye Him, all His angels: praise ye Him, all His hosts. Praise ye Him, sun and moon: praise Him, all ye stars of light. Praise Him, ye heavens of heavens, and ye waters that be above the heavens. Let them praise the name of the Lord: for He commanded, and they were created. He hath also stablished them for ever and ever: He hath made a decree which shall not pass'' (Psalm 148:1—6).

How rich the Lord Jesus was in His possessions, what an estate was His — and what praise He received!

2. He was rich in position:

Not only was the Lord Jesus rich in possessions, but He was rich in His position with the Father. He, *"being in the form of God, thought it not robbery to be equal with God"* (Phil. 2:6).

Jesus was equal with God! He was in the beginning *with* God, He was God in flesh, and in Him dwelt all the fulness of the Godhead bodily. On more than one occasion He told the Pharisees that He was equal with God, and that all He did was done *to the glory* of God.

But He left that glorious position with the Father to come into this world of sin and sorrow, for the express purpose of dying that sinners, through faith in His finished work, might have *life eternal*.

3. He was rich in His Person:

There are no photographs of the Lord Jesus, and I do not believe that any artist has ever touched the hem of the garment in putting His face and features on canvas. Yet every person who met Him recognized Him as being

31

different from other men.

Hebrews 1:3 speaks of Him as being the brightness of God's glory and *"the express image of His Person."* All the holiness that enriched God the Father also enriched His precious Son. He inspired such faith in the woman with the twelve-year issue of blood that she said, "If I may but touch His garment, I shall be whole" (Matt. 9:21). When poor, blind Bartimaeus heard that Jesus was near, he cried out for mercy—"and immediately he received his sight, and followed Jesus in the way" (Mark 10:46–52).

The *demons* recognized Jesus and confessed with fear and trembling that He was the Son of God (Matt. 8:29). When the chief priests and the Pharisees sent officers to arrest Him and the officers returned empty handed, the Pharisees asked, "Why have ye not brought Him?" The officers replied, *"Never man spake like THIS Man!"* (John 7:40–46).

I wish I could have met Him face to face. I wish I could have walked with Him and talked with Him in His earthly ministry. How rich He was in His Person!

4. He was rich in power:

"And Jesus came and spake unto them, saying, ALL power is given unto me in heaven and in earth" (Matt. 28:18). In John 10:18 He said, "No man taketh (my life) from me, but I lay it down of myself. *I have power to lay it down, and I have power to take it again.* This commandment have I received of my Father."

Jesus—Creator of the universe—need but speak a word to *cremate* such a world as ours! He spoke the world into being — what power He holds in His mighty hands! In Revelation 1:13–15 John tells us that His eyes are like flames of fire, and *"His voice as the sound of many waters!"*

Yes, beloved — Jesus was rich in power, yet He surrendered that power and allowed wicked hands of sinful men to nail Him to a cross that you and I might become rich through His grace! One day He will *demonstrate* His mighty power and will give to us, His children, a new heaven and a new earth wherein dwelleth righteousness.

5.　He was rich in worship:

Our Lord was rich in worship from the beginning. Job 38:7 tells us that when Jesus created the universe "the morning stars sang together, and all the sons of God shouted for joy." The angels and all the heavenly beings worship Him and praise His name.

"For the Lord is a great God, and a great King above all gods. . . O come, let us worship and bow down: let us kneel before the Lord our Maker" (Psalm 95:3,6).

". . . The Lord made the heavens. Honour and majesty are before Him: strength and beauty are in His sanctuary. Give unto the Lord, O ye kindreds of the people, give unto the Lord glory and strength. Give unto the Lord the glory due unto His name: bring an offering, and come into His courts. O worship the Lord in the beauty of holiness: fear before Him, all the earth" (Psalm 96:5-9).

There are many, many other Scriptures that tell of the richness of the worship our Lord receives; but He left it all to come to earth—to be rejected, cursed, mocked, ridiculed, spit upon and crucified, that we might be made rich in His marvelous grace!

6.　He was rich in love:

Our Saviour was rich in the love the Father had for Him.　Jesus is the only personality of whom the Father said, *"This is my beloved Son, in whom I am well pleased!"* John 3:35 tells us, *"The Father loveth the Son, and hath given all things into His hand."*

33

Jesus and the Father have been from everlasting. They have been equal, they have been ONE. The only possible way to please God is by loving His Son. Jesus had a position with the Father in all of heaven's glory and richness, but He left it for you and for me. He was rich beyond all human imagination — but He gave it all up to take up His abode in a humble carpenter's home on earth, that you and I might share His riches in glory through all eternity. He surrendered all that He had in heaven, that He might take upon Himself the form of sinful man—a form of flesh like yours and mine—and do for us what we could never have done within ourselves:

"For by grace are ye saved through faith; and that not of yourselves: it is the gift of God: *Not of works, lest any man should boast*" (Eph. 2:8,9).

HE BECAME POOR FOR OUR SAKES

Jesus said to His disciples, "*The foxes have holes, and the birds of the air have nests; but the Son of man hath not where to lay His head*" (Matt. 8:20). A person who "has not where to lay his head" reminds us of poverty in greatest degree. We have the poor with us always (Matt. 26:11); but how many people do we know who are so poor they have no place to lay their head when the sun goes down—no roof to shelter them?

Let us study the poverty the Lord Jesus accepted in order to keep sinners out of hell through the riches of His grace. We will appreciate salvation more when we see the great contrast between the riches He had with the Father, and the poverty He accepted to become Saviour of mankind:

1. He became poor in possessions:

Consider the home into which Jesus was born. How much of this world's goods did Mary and Joseph have?

34

Our Lord was not born in a mansion nor in a well-equipped hospital. He was not laid in a soft bed amid silks and fine linen. The circumstances surrounding His birth were the most humble ever recorded in the pages of history: He was born in a sheep barn, wrapped in swaddling clothes, and His first baby-crib was a manger! He stepped from the splendor of heaven to the poverty of earth that WE might step from sin to salvation. He exchanged the singing of the angels for the bleating of sheep, and He grew up in the home of a humble carpenter. I do not doubt that He followed the carpenter trade before He came on the scene of His public ministry.

On one occasion, two of John's disciples asked Jesus where He lived, and He invited, "Come and see." They accepted His invitation, and the Scripture tells us that "they abode with Him that day" (John 1:38,39). I do not know where He took them. Perhaps He led them to a secluded spot where He loved to go and pray. Perhaps they spent the day in the home of friends. Certainly the Lord could not have taken them to His own home, for He had none on earth. He did not even have money to pay His taxes, and He said to Peter, "Go thou to the sea, and cast an hook, and take up the fish that first cometh up; and when thou hast opened his mouth, thou shalt find a piece of money: that take, and give unto them for me and thee" (Matt. 17:27).

Yes, beloved — Jesus stepped from heaven's splendor and riches to the poverty of earth, that WE through His poverty might become rich!

2. He became poor in glory:

Jesus left the glory He had with the Father. He stepped from the ivory palaces into this poor, wretched world of sin. Only a meager few recognized and acknowl-

35

edged His birth, and for many years He was unknown and unheralded by man.

"*He was in the world . . . and the world knew Him not. He came unto His own, and His own received Him not*" (John 1:10,11). Even when the crowds followed and acclaimed Him in the early days of His public ministry, they followed Him only for gain—for the loaves and fishes, for the healing of their bodies, for the spectacular miracles He performed. *They were not there when He was nailed to the cross!*

3.   He became poor in praise:

Our Saviour was the object of heaven's praise when He was with the Father; but when He stepped from heaven to earth, praise turned to curses! Study the Gospels — they tell the story.

People blasphemed Him, they criticized Him, they said He did miracles by the power of Beelzebub, they called Him everything dirty and filthy, they even said He was born out of wedlock. They spat on Him, they whipped Him, they crowned Him with thorns, nailed Him to a cross, and mocked Him as He died!

Oh yes! He became poor—for US. He took our place and paid sin's awful penalty that we might have life, and have it abundantly. Honor and praise were not His upon earth — and I might add that we who *serve* Him will receive very little praise and honor from man.

In His Sermon on the Mount Jesus said, "Blessed are ye, when men shall revile you, and persecute you, and shall say all manner of evil against you falsely, *for my sake.* Rejoice, and be exceeding glad: for great is your reward in heaven: for so persecuted they the prophets which were before you" (Matt. 5:11,12).

To His disciples He said, "If the world hate you, ye

know that it hated me before it hated you. If ye were of the world, the world would love his own: but because ye are not of the world, but I have chosen you out of the world, therefore the world hateth you. . . If they have persecuted me, they will also persecute you. . . . But all these things will they do unto you for my name's sake, because they know not Him that sent me" (John 15:18–21).

In II Timothy 3:12 we are assured that "all who will live godly in Christ Jesus shall suffer persecution!" And in I Peter 4:12,13 we are told, "Beloved, think it not strange concerning the fiery trial which is to try you, as though some strange thing happened unto you: but rejoice, *inasmuch as ye are partakers of Christ's sufferings . . . ."*

The hatred the world had for Jesus is extended to those who will follow Him in spirit and in truth. He had no praise of men.

4. He became poor in His Person:

From the riches of His Person with the Father, Jesus stepped to the poverty of a person among men. He was the express image of the Father, He was full of grace and truth; but men did not recognize Him as such.

They admitted that He had no sin. They admitted that "never man spake" like THIS Man spoke. They did not deny that He taught with authority, and not as the scribes. Pilate thrice confessed that he could find no fault in Jesus. Yet His enemies accused Him of being in partnership with the devil. They said He cast out devils by the *power* of the devil. They hired false witnesses to testify against Him at His trial. They *would not* admit that He was the Son of God!

His back was cut with the Roman lashes, His beard plucked out by the roots. His head was crowned with a crown of thorns, His hands and feet were torn with the spikes that nailed Him to the cross. His side was pierced with a Roman spear.

He died the most shameful death known in His day — and He died that death that you and I might be spared the eternal death of the sinner. It is through HIS death that WE have life. It is through His poverty that the riches of His grace are made possible for US.

Do you want to KNOW Him, sinner? Do you APPRE-CIATE Him, Christian?

5. He was poor in His separation from God:

As the Lord Jesus hung on the cross, He became poor in His separation from the Father. During His earthly ministry He was in close relationship with God every step of the way; but when the sins of the world were placed on Him at Calvary, He cried in agony, *"My God! My God! Why hast thou forsaken me?"*

God literally turned His back on Jesus while He paid the penalty for your sins and mine. A holy God cannot look upon sin, and His Son was paying the sin-debt for the whole world—past, present, and future. He paid a tremendous price for our salvation; He paid with every drop of His precious blood. But more than that, He paid by not being able to see His Father's face nor feel His Father's presence.

Thank God for the poverty of Jesus in behalf of my poor soul! Have YOU accepted the riches of His grace? If not, won't you do it right now? Think of the Lord Jesus dying on Calvary for you. Realize what a price He paid for your salvation. Won't you accept His wonderful provision for your soul right now, and become rich in His grace?

LET US FOLLOW THE PATH OF HIS HUMILIATION

"Let this mind be in you, which was also in Christ Jesus: Who, being in the form of God, thought it not robbery to be equal with God: But made Himself of no reputation, and took upon Him the form of a servant, and was made in the likeness of men: And being found in fashion as a man, He humbled Himself, and became obedient unto death, even the death of the cross" (Phil. 2:5–8).

Jesus came from God. His beginning was not at His birth in Bethlehem — He had been throughout all eternity with God; and many times during His public ministry He *declared* that He came from the Father:

"For the bread of God is He which cometh down from heaven, and giveth life unto the world" (John 6:33).

"For I came down from heaven, not to do mine own will, but the will of Him that sent me" (John 6:38).

"I am that bread of life. Your fathers did eat manna in the wilderness, and are dead. This is the bread which cometh down from heaven, that a man may eat thereof, and not die. I am the living bread which came down from heaven: if any man eat of this bread, he shall live for ever: and the bread that I will give is my flesh, which I will give for the life of the world" (John 6:48–51).

In John 8:14 He said, "Though I bear record of myself, yet my record is true: for I know whence I came, and whither I go; but ye cannot tell whence I come, and whither I go."

"In John 8:42 He declared, ". . . I proceeded forth and came from God; neither came I of myself, but He sent me."

There was no doubt in the mind of Jesus as to where He came from. He KNEW He was God incarnate in flesh.

He knew His mission when He left the ivory palaces of the Father's house. He knew when He left the singing of the angels that He would be cursed by the angry religious leaders of His day. Yet knowing all that, He did not shrink from doing the will of God the Father.

Jesus was set at nought by men from the cradle to the grave. The world did not honor Him in His birth, it hated Him in life, it disowned Him in death. He knew all of this would happen when He left the Father's bosom — yet He was willing to become poor that sinners might be saved. God said, "The soul that sinneth, it shall die" (Ezek. 18:4), and it was necessary for one to take the place of sinners and pay sin's penalty.

JESUS DIED A CRIMINAL'S DEATH

He became obedient unto death—*"even the death of the cross!"* The most hardened criminals died in that manner. Thus Jesus died the most shameful death possible. He was paying the greatest debt ever paid.

On Calvary He stepped to the lowest depths of His humiliation. He was numbered among criminals and thieves. He was slain as an imposter and a blasphemer. He was the Prince of Peace — yet He was put to death as a *disturber* of the peace. He was led as a lamb to the slaughter, and "as a sheep before her shearers is dumb, so He openeth not His mouth" (Isa. 53:7).

WITH GOD, THE WAY UP IS DOWN

Jesus stepped to the depths of humiliation. Now let us follow His path of *exaltation*:

"Wherefore God also hath highly exalted Him, and given Him a name which is above every name: That at the name of Jesus every knee should bow, of things in heaven, and things in earth, and things under the earth;

40

and that every tongue should confess that Jesus Christ is Lord, to the glory of God the Father" (Phil. 2:9–11).

Yes, the way UP, with God, is DOWN. ". . . God resisteth the proud, and giveth grace to the humble. Humble yourselves therefore under the mighty hand of God, that He may exalt you in due time" (I Pet. 5:5,6).

Jesus never questioned the Father's will for Him while He was on earth. He *came into the world* to do the Father's will; and if WE would follow the Lord, listen to His voice and do as He bids us do, *all heaven would be at our disposal!*

The steps of our Lord's exaltation are as *glorious* as the steps of His humiliation were *humbling*. He has been exalted in degree as He was humbled. His enemies wagged their heads and mocked Him while He died on the cross; but it was quite another story when the empty tomb was discovered early on the first day of the week. They denied everything He said while He was here on earth. They shouted, "He saved others — Himself He cannot save!" They thought it was the end for Him when He cried out and gave up the ghost — but they learned differently when the guards came running, telling them what had happened when the angel came and rolled away the stone from the tomb.   The Lord's resurrection could not be explained away — it was proof of everything He said during His earthly ministry.

The scribes and Pharisees said to Him, "Master, we would see a SIGN from thee." He replied, "An evil and adulterous generation seeketh after a sign; and there shall no sign be given to it, but the sign of the prophet Jonas: For as Jonas was three days and three nights in the whale's belly; so shall the Son of man be three days and three nights in the heart of the earth" (Matt. 12:38–40).

41

He told them He would spend three days and nights in the heart of the earth and then come forth, and He did exactly what He said He would do. He declared, "I have power to lay my life down, and I have power to take it again." He laid His life down and He took it up again just as He said He would do.

Had the Lord Jesus remained in the grave, all that He said and taught would have died with Him and the riches of His grace would never have been known. Paul tells us that our faith and our preaching would be in vain had not Christ risen from the dead. Everything depended upon His conquering of death; and when He broke the bonds of death and came forth, He proved Himself the Son of God with power. The greatest bombshell ever to explode in the face of an unbelieving world was the resurrection of the Lord Jesus Christ!

After His glorious resurrection He appeared to His disciples and others of the saints for forty days. Some were slow to believe that He was really the Christ of God, but even doubting Thomas became convinced that this was truly the resurrected Lord.

In Acts 1:1—11 we read:

"The former treatise have I made, O Theophilus, of all that Jesus began both to do and teach, until the day in which He was taken up, after that He through the Holy Ghost had given commandments unto the apostles whom He had chosen: To whom also He shewed Himself alive after His passion by many infallible proofs, being seen of them forty days, and speaking of the things pertaining to the kingdom of God: And, being assembled together with them, commanded them that they should not depart from Jerusalem, but wait for the promise of the Father, which, saith He, ye have heard of me. For John truly baptized with water; but ye shall be baptized with the Holy Ghost not many days hence.

"When they therefore were come together, they asked of Him, saying, Lord, wilt thou at this time restore again the kingdom to Israel? And He said unto them, It is not for you to know the times or the seasons, which the Father hath put in His own power. But ye shall receive power, after that the Holy Ghost is come upon you: and ye shall be witnesses unto me both in Jerusalem, and in all Judaea, and in Samaria, and unto the uttermost part of the earth.

"And when He had spoken these things, while they beheld, He was taken up; and a cloud received Him out of their sight. And while they looked stedfastly toward heaven as He went up, behold, two men stood by them in white apparel; which also said, Ye men of Galilee, why stand ye gazing up into heaven? This same Jesus, which is taken up from you into heaven, shall so come in like manner as ye have seen Him go into heaven."

His glorious ascension! How different from the hour when Joseph and Nicodemus took His lifeless, wounded body from the cross, wrapped it in grave clothes, laid it in the tomb and rolled a stone against the entrance; and soldiers secured the entrance with the Roman seal.

But in Matthew 28:2 we read, ". . . The angel of the Lord descended from heaven, and came and rolled back the stone from the door, and sat upon it." To Mary Magdalene and "the other Mary" the angel said, "Fear not ye: for I know that ye seek Jesus, which was crucified. He is not here: *for He is risen, AS HE SAID.*"

Yes, Jesus was everything He claimed to be—and He proved it!

With my spiritual eye I can see Him as He ascended out of sight as His followers gazed with amazement into the vastness of the sky. I can see Him as He passed on up, up — beyond all the planets, through the great solar systems — and then I see the heavenly host as they awaited Him at heaven's door, to welcome Him back home!

I can easily imagine that all the angels sang as the Son of God entered again the heavenly abode which He had left more than thirty years before, to take upon Himself the form of man, to conquer sin and death, that men might be saved from hell.

With my spiritual ear I can hear the praises that fill all heaven as the Son is seated at the right hand of the Father—the exalted place He left to descend into this sin-benighted world to die for you and me.

In Hebrews 1:3 we are told that "when He had by Himself purged our sins, (He) sat down on the right hand of the Majesty on high." Thank God, our Saviour has been exalted to His eternal position with God the Father!

But even though He was resurrected, even though He ascended to heaven, and even though He is now seated at the right hand of God, there is one step yet to be taken in His exaltation:

He came the first time as a babe in a manger, as a Lamb for sacrifice. He was rejected, despised, humiliated, and put to death. But He is *coming again* — and when He comes the second time it will be in great power and great glory. He will come as King of kings and Lord of lords. He will be "revealed from heaven with His mighty angels, in flaming fire taking vengeance on them that know not God, and that obey not the Gospel of our Lord Jesus Christ: Who shall be punished with everlasting destruction from the presence of the Lord, and from the glory of His power" (II Thess. 1:7–9).

Christ is coming again, and from all indications that coming is very near. He is coming to reign until He has put all enemies under His royal feet! He will deal the final blow to Satan and his works. He will sit on the throne of His father David in Jerusalem, and for one

44

thousand glorious years He will reign over this earth—and the saints of God will reign with Him. He will then reign FOREVER as the exalted One of God.

Yes, Jesus left the ivory palaces and the riches of heaven, and became poor for our sakes, that we, through faith in Him, might share the riches of God's grace. But if we would share the crown with Him, we must follow Him as He commands in His Word. He set the example, and in Matthew 10:38 He said, "He that taketh not his cross, and followeth after me, is not worthy of me." Cross-bearing will not save us, it has nothing to do with our salvation; but it has *everything* to do with our receiving a full reward in our inheritance at the end of life's journey.

In Hebrews 13:11—13 we read, "For the bodies of those beasts, whose blood is brought into the sanctuary by the high priest for sin, are burned without the camp. *Wherefore Jesus also, that He might sanctify the people with His own blood, suffered without the gate. Let us go forth therefore unto Him without the camp, bearing His reproach!*" I wonder how much reproach we have suffered for Him?

Romans 8:17 tells us that if we are children of God we are also His heirs—"heirs of God, and joint-heirs with Christ; if so be that we suffer with Him, that we may be also glorified together." The question is: "ARE YOU A CHILD OF GOD?" If you are His child, you have a perfect right to claim every promise the Bible makes to God's children. But if you are just a church member, if you "have religion" but lack salvation, you will one day hear Him say to the angels, "Bind him hand and foot and cast him into outer darkness, where there is weeping and wailing and gnashing of teeth!"

The only way to become a child of God is to be saved

45

by grace through faith in Jesus: "Neither is there salvation in any other: for there is none other name under heaven given among men, whereby we must be saved" (Acts 4:12).

Jesus Himself declared, "I am the way, the truth, and the life. No man cometh unto the Father but by me." Beloved reader, if you want to share the riches of His grace, you MUST accept His death, burial, and resurrection. If you would reign with Him, you must be willing to suffer with Him. If you would share His crown in glory, you must be willing to bear the cross in this life.

"Thanks be unto God for His unspeakable gift" (II Cor. 9:15). I am so glad that years ago I accepted Him on the terms of the Gospel and He saved my soul! I can truthfully say that I have never seen the day I wanted to turn back to the old life and the beggarly elements of the world. I have found real life, joy, and peace in Jesus.

If YOU do not know Him, bow your head and trust Him right now. If you DO know Him, bow your head and thank Him again that "though He was rich, yet for our sakes He became poor; that through His poverty we might be made rich!"

CHRIST BARE OUR SINS

CHRIST BARE OUR SINS

"Who His own self bare our sins in His own body on the tree, that we, being dead to sins, should live unto righteousness: by whose stripes ye were healed. For ye were as sheep going astray; but are now returned unto the Shepherd and Bishop of your souls" (1 Pet. 2:24,25).

The Lord Jesus Christ did not trust angels, cherubim, or any other heavenly creature to bear our sins, but HIMSELF bore our sins in His own body on the cross —not because HE had sinned, for He was the sinless One; but He bore OUR sins that we, being dead to sin, should live unto righteousness. By HIS stripes *we were* (past tense) HEALED!

In our text we find the *nature*, the *design*, the *need*, and the *results* of the atonement purchased by Jesus at the tremendous price of His own blood, shed willingly on the cross. Let us look first at the nature of the atonement.

I.
The NATURE of the Blood Atonement

The Hebrew word translated "pitch" is our English word "atonement," and it occurs in the Bible first in Genesis 6:14, where the Lord said unto Noah, "Make thee an ark of gopher wood; rooms shalt thou make in the ark, and shalt pitch it within and without with pitch."

It is common knowledge that boats must be watertight and leakproof or they will sink. It was the pitch within and without the ark that made it unsinkable.

God looked down upon the earth and saw the wickedness of man, "and it repented the Lord that He had made man on the earth, and it grieved Him at His heart. And the Lord said, I will destroy man whom I have created from the face of the earth; both man, and beast, and the creeping thing, and the fowls of the air; for it repenteth me that I have made them. *But Noah found grace in the eyes of the Lord"* (Gen. 6:6—8).

Noah believed what God had said, thus he found grace in the eyes of the Lord, and to him God gave the blueprints and specifications for building the ark. Noah obeyed God, and in the last verse of Genesis 6 we read, "Thus did Noah; according to ALL THAT GOD COMMANDED HIM, so did he." And in Genesis 7:1, "the Lord said unto Noah, *Come thou* and all thy house into the ark; for thee have I seen righteous before me in this generation."

The invitation *"Come thou"* proves that God was *already inside* the ark. He had inspected it, He found that Noah had followed specifications to the letter, the ark was pitched inside and out with pitch, it was safe—and God invited Noah to come in.

Thus we have the picture of atonement. But now just suppose that you and I had never heard the words of our text before in all of our lives. Just suppose that we had no religious prejudice and no preconceived ideas or opinions concerning the shed blood of Jesus and the atonement. What would we gain from these tremendous words?

"Who His own self bare our sins in His own body on the tree." Could it be stated more plainly? Are there any words that could break this statement down into a more understandable form? In this clear, concise statement we immediately see the vicarious, substitutionary sufferings and death of the Lamb of God who took the sinner's place and paid the sin-debt. Scholars tell us that "when a king graciously allows one person who is under no obligation whatsoever to do so, to discharge a

50

service or suffer punishment for another on whom such obligation rests, THAT IS SUBSTITUTION. And when that service is discharged by the one willing but under no obligation, when that penalty is suffered by the substitute, the service or the suffering becomes VICARIOUS."

God the Father, sovereign God of heaven and earth, graciously allowed Jesus Christ to become our substitute and take our place. He was under no obligation whatsoever because HE had committed no sin; but God the Father turned His head while Jesus suffered death, the penalty for sin, and became our Saviour because of His substitutionary suffering for our sins.

The atonement of Christ is therefore substitutionary and vicarious—a truth confirmed and clearly taught in the Old Testament. The entire sacrificial system under the Mosaic Law pointed to the work and the shed blood of Christ Jesus. God's representative who offered the sacrifice first laid his hand on the head of the victim which was to BE sacrificed, and confessed his sins over it. By so doing he identified himself with it in the first instance and transferred his sins to the victim in the second instance.

This is a perfect picture of substitution and vicarious atonement. There is no contradiction in the teaching of the prophets concerning the substitutionary and vicarious atonement purchased by Jesus' blood.

Let Isaiah Testify

It was prophesied centuries before the birth of Jesus that He would be wounded, bruised, whipped, and crucified—the innocent suffering for the guilty, the righteous dying for the unrighteous, in order that God the Father could be just and yet justify the ungodly through the substitutionary and vicarious atonement of the Son:

51

"Who hath believed our report? and to whom is the arm of the Lord revealed? For He shall grow up before Him as a tender plant, and as a root out of a dry ground: He hath no form nor comeliness; and when we shall see Him, there is no beauty that we should desire Him. He is despised and rejected of men; a man of sorrows, and acquainted with grief: and we hid as it were our faces from Him; He was despised, and we esteemed Him not. Surely He hath borne our griefs, and carried our sorrows: yet we did esteem Him stricken, smitten of God, and afflicted. But He was wounded for our transgressions, He was bruised for our iniquities: the chastisement of our peace was upon Him; and with His stripes we are healed.

"All we like sheep have gone astray; we have turned every one to his own way; and the Lord hath laid on Him the iniquity of us all.

"He was oppressed, and He was afflicted, yet He opened not His mouth: He is brought as a lamb to the slaughter, and as a sheep before her shearers is dumb, so He openeth not His mouth. He was taken from prison and from judgment: and who shall declare His generation? for He was cut off out of the land of the living: for the transgression of my people was He stricken. And He made His grave with the wicked, and with the rich in His death; because He had done no violence, neither was any deceit in His mouth.

"Yet it pleased the Lord to bruise Him; He hath put Him to grief: when thou shalt make His soul an offering for sin, He shall see His seed, He shall prolong His days, and the pleasure of the Lord shall prosper in His hand. He shall see of the travail of His soul, and shall be satisfied: by His knowledge shall my righteous servant justify many; for He shall bear their iniquities. Therefore will I divide Him a portion with the great, and He shall divide the spoil with the strong; because He hath poured out His soul unto death: and He was numbered with the transgressors; and He bare the sin of many, and made intercession for the transgressors" (Isaiah 53).

Let David Testify

The thirty-second Psalm is a commentary on the vicarious suffering of Jesus. Please read the entire chapter; time and space permit us to give only the first two verses here: "Blessed is he whose transgression is forgiven, whose sin is covered. Blessed is the man unto whom the Lord imputeth not iniquity, and in whose spirit there is no guile."

Let the Apostle Paul Testify

Paul was called and commissioned a minister to the Gentiles, and sent to the Church with the Gospel of the marvelous grace of God. In the fourth chapter of Romans he quotes the words of David in the Psalm just given, thus assuring us that even *David* understood the great truth of the substitution and vicarious suffering of the innocent for the guilty. David looked *forward* to the cross; we on this side of Calvary look *back* to the cross. From Genesis 3:15 through Revelation 22 it is the substitutionary and vicarious atonement that makes peace between the hell-bound sinner and a holy God:

"For what saith the Scripture? Abraham believed God, and it was counted unto him for righteousness. Now to him that worketh is the reward not reckoned of grace, but of debt. But to him that worketh not, but believeth on Him that justifieth the ungodly, his faith is counted for righteousness. Even as David also describeth the blessedness of the man, unto whom God imputeth righteousness without works, saying, Blessed are they whose iniquities are forgiven, and whose sins are covered. Blessed is the man to whom the Lord will not impute sin" (Rom. 4:3–8).

According to Paul's further testimony, given in Romans 3:21–28, when we add up everything the answer is that *man*, who deserves to die (because all have sinned and come short of the glory of God), is *justified by faith* without the deeds of the law, through the redemption that is in Christ Jesus. God's Christ became man's Jesus. God set Him forth to be a propitiation through faith in His blood, to declare God's righteousness for the remission for sins that are past—sins from Eden to Calvary—that were passed over by God through His forbearance. But since we are justified by the blood of Jesus through faith in His finished work, all boasting is excluded. We have nothing to boast *about*! *We are made righteous because of His substitutionary and vicarious death.*

"Christ hath redeemed us from the curse of the law, being made a curse for us: for it is written, Cursed is every one that hangeth on a tree" (Gal. 3:13). Please notice that the redemption is already accomplished: "Christ HATH redeemed us." It happened when He bore our sins in His own body on the tree.

Christ died for every sinner, and whosoever believeth that Jesus is the Christ has this redemption. Christ was made a curse for us, and through His cursed, shameful death we are made sons of God, heirs of God, joint-heirs with Jesus Christ.

Now Hear the Testimony of Jesus

One day the mother of James and John came to Jesus with a very special request. She said, "Grant that these my two sons may sit, the one on thy right hand, and the other on the left, in thy kingdom." Jesus replied, "Ye know not what ye ask . . . to sit on my right hand, and on my left, is not mine to give, but it shall be given to them for whom it is prepared of my Father. . . Whosoever will be great among you, let him be your minister; and whosoever will be chief among you, let him be your servant:

54

Even as the Son of man came not to be ministered unto, but to minister, and to give His life a ransom for many" (Matt. 20:20—28 in part).

In spite of all that preachers, teachers, evangelists, and writers have said about Jesus, it can be summed up in the words we have just read. He came to minister, and to give His life a ransom for many. He came to lay His life down that we who deserve to die might live by exercising faith in His shed blood. Hear Him again in John 10:17,18: "Therefore doth my Father love me, because I lay down my life, that I might take it again. No man taketh it from me, but I lay it down of myself. I have power to lay it down, and I have power to take it again. This commandment have I received of my Father."

That is what He came into the world to do. He came to lay HIS life down that WE might have life through believing in His finished work. That is the way it had to be in order that God might be just and yet justify the ungodly. It was God the Father who loved us in the beginning. Before He created one grain of the dust from which He made Adam, He thought and perfected redemption — and Peter plainly tells us when, who, and how:

"Forasmuch as ye know that ye were not redeemed with corruptible things, as silver and gold, from your vain conversation received by tradition from your fathers; but with the precious blood of Christ, as of a lamb without blemish and without spot: who verily was foreordained before the foundation of the world, but was manifest in these last times for you. Who by Him do believe in God, that raised Him up from the dead, and gave Him glory; that your faith and hope might be in God. . . Being born again, not of corruptible seed, but of incorruptible, by the Word of God, which liveth and abideth for ever"

(I Pet. 1:18–23).

Remember

"For He (God) hath made Him (Jesus) to be sin for us (for you and me), who (Jesus) knew no sin; that we might be made the righteousness of God in Him" (II Cor. 5:21).

My finite mind cannot grasp the wonder of those words. I cannot understand how God could love so much. Sovereign God, the God of all creation, God of heaven and earth and all that is therein, Father of our Lord and Saviour Jesus Christ, could destroy the entire universe with but a word. Yet it was that same sovereign God who so loved me, a poor, hell-deserving sinner, that He made His only begotten Son to be sin for ME! Jesus did not *commit* sin, there was no sin IN Him; but God made Him to BE sin for us, that we might be made the righteousness of God in Him.

We do not become the righteousness of God through a process of living, giving, or doing. But when we believe on the Lord Jesus Christ and put our faith in His finished work, that instant we are made the righteousness of God in HIM.

The Sufferings of the Son Satisfied the Holiness of the Father

We know that God the Father is completely satisfied with the Son. A heavenly host announced His birth. God the Father audibly announced Him as HIS SON when He was baptized. On the Mount of Transfiguration, God the Father again spoke in an audible voice, declaring, "This is my beloved Son, in whom I am well pleased. Hear ye Him." And on a third occasion (John 12:28,29) God spoke concerning His Son. "The people therefore, that stood by, and heard it, said that it thundered: others said, An

56

angel spake to Him."

We know that Jesus fully satisfied the Father in every detail of His ministry, His death, and His resurrection, because He is now seated in the highest seat of heaven, at the right hand of the Majesty. He has been glorified with the Father with the same glory He had before He took the sinner's place and became our substitute. In John 17:5 Jesus prayed, "And now, O Father, glorify thou me with thine own self with the glory which I had with thee before the world was!"

Paul sheds more light on the Saviour's glorification in Hebrews 12:2:

". . . Who for the joy that was set before Him endured the cross, despising the shame, and is set down at the right hand of the throne of God."

Please notice — Jesus did not enjoy the cross; but for the joy that was set before Him, joy that would be His on the other side of Calvary, He was willing to *endure* the cross and bear the shame because He knew that when He *finished* the work the Father had assigned Him to do, He would again be seated at the Father's right hand.

"God, who at sundry times and in divers manners spake in time past unto the fathers by the prophets, hath in these last days spoken unto us by His Son, whom He hath appointed heir of all things, by whom also He made the worlds; who being the brightness of His glory, and the express image of His person, and upholding all things by the word of His power, when He had by Himself purged our sins, sat down on the right hand of the Majesty on high" (Heb. 1:1–3).

And from His seat at the right hand of God He makes intercession for us — the only One who CAN mediate between us and God:

"For there is one God, and *one Mediator* between God and men, the Man Christ Jesus" (I Tim. 2:5).

II.
The Divine DESIGN of the Atonement

"That we, being dead to sins, should live unto right-eousness." Here we see the twofold design of the atonement. God gave Jesus not only to take away our guilt, but also to change our lives; not only to take away the wages of sin, but to put within us divine nature and make us new creations in Christ Jesus. Thus, the divine design of the atonement is both negative and positive:

"For the love of Christ constraineth us; because we thus judge, that if One died for all, then were all dead: and that He died for all, that they which live should not henceforth live unto themselves, but unto Him which died for them, and rose again. . . Therefore if any man be in Christ, he is a new creature: old things are passed away; behold, all things are become new" (II Cor. 5:14–17).

". . . Being dead to sins . . . ." It may be impossible for us to fully comprehend the meaning of this statement, but we have here almost the same statement used in Romans 6:1–10 with reference to Christ our Saviour; and if we can understand the meaning of the words as having to do with HIM, we may, in that understanding, find the meaning for our own individual hearts.

Christ "died unto sin once," which means that in the sense that sin was responsible for His crucifixion, when once He paid the penalty (the wages of sin) by dying, sin lost forever the power to bring Him into the place of its penalty again. A debt paid in full can never be paid again. Therefore *Jesus* "died to sin"—not HIS sin, for He was sinless; but OUR sin which He bore in His own body on the cross.

58

By way of illustration, if a person commits premeditated murder, he is given a fair trial, a jury of twelve citizens finds him guilty, and due penalty is assessed. When that guilty individual *pays* the penalty and serves his sentence, his debt to society is paid and he can never again be brought into judgment for that crime.

JESUS was not guilty, but He died FOR the guilty. He took the guilty sinner's place and died *once*, never to die again. He was dead, He is alive forevermore, seated at the right hand of God the Father (Rev. 1:18; I Tim. 2:5).

The Believer Is Identified With Christ

The born again believer is so thoroughly identified with Christ that he stands before God just as though he had never sinned. He stands before God *IN CHRIST*, our Representative and our Substitute. When Christ died on the cross, He died to sin; the believer also *died with Him*.

Paul gives testimony to this Bible truth in Galatians 2:20: "I am crucified with Christ: nevertheless I live; yet not I, but Christ liveth in me: and the life which I now live in the flesh I live by the faith of the Son of God, who loved me, and gave Himself for me."

Therefore, since sin cannot again bring the believer's *Substitute* into the place of sin's penalty, since He who died for the sinner can die no more, neither can the one who is *represented IN* the death of Jesus be brought again under the penalty of sin:

"There is therefore now no condemnation to them which are in Christ Jesus, who walk not after the flesh, but after the Spirit" (Rom. 8:1).

This statement is not difficult to understand. It simply means that no guilt, no penalty, no judgment rests upon the believer because he is IN CHRIST. Believers sit together in heavenly places in Christ Jesus, in Him we are identified, and He stands with us, our Substitute: "Even the mystery which hath been hid from ages and from generations, but now is made manifest to His saints: To whom God would make known what is the riches of the glory of this mystery among the Gentiles; *which is Christ in YOU, the hope of glory"* (Col. 1:26,27).

"What shall we then say to these things? If God be for us, who can be against us? He that spared not His own Son, but delivered Him up for us all, how shall He not with Him also freely give us all things? Who shall lay anything to the charge of God's elect? It is God that justifieth. Who is he that condemneth? It is Christ that died, yea rather, that is risen again, who is even at the right hand of God, who also maketh intercession for us.

"Who shall separate us from the love of Christ? Shall tribulation, or distress, or persecution, or famine, or nakedness, or peril, or sword? As it is written, For thy sake we are killed all the day long; we are accounted as sheep for the slaughter. Nay, in all these things we are more than conquerors through Him that loved us. For I am persuaded, that neither death, nor life, nor angels, nor principalities, nor powers, nor things present, nor things to come, nor height, nor depth, nor any other creature, shall be able to separate us from the love of God, which is in Christ Jesus our Lord" (Rom. 8:31—39).

Christ not only bore our SIN (singular), but also our SINS (plural). He bore the SIN of unbelief that would damn us, and He bore the SINS that would rob the believer of his peace, joy, and reward. It takes only one sin—the sin of unbelief—to damn the soul. We are born sinners, and until we believe on the Lord Jesus Christ we *remain* sinners.

"He that believeth on Him is not condemned: but he that believeth not is condemned already, because he hath not believed in the name of the only begotten Son of God" (John 3:18).

The tree of unbelief bears many kinds of fruit. Jesus bore our SIN, and He also bore our SINS. John testifies to this in I John 1:7: "If we walk in the light, as HE is in the light, we have fellowship one with another, and the blood of Jesus Christ His Son cleanseth us from all sin." Again, in I John 2:1,2 we read, "My little children, these things write I unto you, that ye sin not. And if any man sin, we have an Advocate with the Father, Jesus Christ the righteous: and He is the propitiation for our sins: and not for our's only, but also for the sins of the whole world."

The blood of Jesus Christ does not redeem us and then leave us to *keep* ourselves redeemed. The blood cleanses — and *continues* to cleanse. If Christians sin, we have an Advocate with the Father; and if we confess our sins, our faithful and just Advocate will forgive us. When we are truly saved, in the eyes of God we stand just as just as Jesus is just. We stand before God just as pure as the blood that covers us.

The design of the atonement goes beyond the negative. It is true that we are *dead to sin*, and we have the promise, "If any man be in Christ Jesus, he is a new creation." We know there is no condemnation to those who are in Christ Jesus; and we know the blood of Jesus Christ cleanses from all sin. But in its *positive* design the atonement puts within us *divine nature*:

"Whereby are given unto us exceeding great and precious promises: that by these ye might be partakers of the divine nature, having escaped the corruption that is in the world through lust" (II Pet. 1:4).

"Except a man be born of water and OF THE SPIRIT, he cannot enter into the kingdom of God" (John 3:5).

"But ye are not in the flesh, but in the Spirit, if so be that the Spirit of God dwell in you. Now if any man have not the Spirit of Christ, he is none of His" (Rom. 8:9).

"For as many as are led by the Spirit of God, they are the sons of God. . . The Spirit itself beareth witness with our spirit, that we are the children of God" (Rom. 8:14,16).

"And grieve not the Holy Spirit of God, *whereby ye are sealed* unto the day of redemption" (Eph. 4:30).

Believers have the gift of the Holy Spirit with all the operations of His grace within us. The moment we receive the Lord Jesus Christ by faith, the Holy Spirit takes up His abode within us. He regenerates us, creates within us a new man, a new heart, and leads us into the paths of right living (Psalm 23:3).

This does not mean that even the *most dedicated* believer will not be tempted and tested by Satan. As long as we remain in this earth we *will* be tempted; but we have the promise of I Corinthians 10:13:

"There hath no temptation taken you but such as is common to man: but God is faithful, who will not suffer you to be tempted above that ye are able; but will with the temptation also make a way to escape, that ye may be able to bear it."

To be *"dead to sin"* means that through the miracle of the new birth and the power of the Holy Spirit sin's power over us is broken, and sin shall not have dominion over us.

The positive aspect of the atonement is that Christ died—not just to deliver us from sin, that we should be dead to sin judicially and experimentally, *but that we might LIVE UNTO RIGHTEOUSNESS.*

Believers live right because they have been made right in their hearts. They love righteousness because they have a new nature within. "That which is born of the Spirit IS spirit," and therefore the Holy Spirit leads the Christian into paths of right living.

In Romans 6:5 Paul tells us that we are united with Christ in the likeness of His death; and since this is true, we are also united with Him in the likeness of His resurrection. *All believers died to sin* when Jesus died on the cross; and since we died with Him, we shall also *live* with Him. The moment we receive Him as Saviour we experience the miracle made possible on Calvary.

In the atonement Jesus not only provided that we shall live with Him *in heaven FOREVER*, but also that we should live *with* Him and *for* Him NOW, in a spiritual state of resurrection glory. We do not yet have our glorified bodies, but we DO have *a new creation within*. Jesus died unto sin once, but the life He now lives He lives unto God; and we are likewise to reckon ourselves dead unto sin and alive unto God in Christ Jesus (Rom. 6:11).

Every born again believer possesses eternal life now: "Beloved, NOW are we the sons of God . . ." (I John 3:2). We sit together in heavenly places in Christ Jesus NOW (Eph. 2:6,7). We are dead, and our lives are hid with Christ in God NOW (Col. 3:3). But even though we are dead, *we LIVE* — we live unto Christ. To the believer, death (the wages of sin) is past, and glory is in the future!

Because the believer possesses the Holy Spirit, righteousness has been imputed by faith — and he therefore no longer follows the path of death and darkness, yielding his members as servants of unrighteousness unto iniquity. Instead, he is servant to righteousness unto holiness.

The believer not only puts off *the old man* with his deeds, "anger, wrath, malice, blasphemy, filthy communication." He also puts ON "the *new man* which is renewed

63

in knowledge after the image of Him that created him . . .
mercies, kindness, humbleness of mind, meekness, longsuffering . . . and above all these things . . . *charity*, which
is the bond of perfectness" (Col. 3:8–14 in part). Every
true believer can say, "By HIS stripes I am healed—*perfect-
ly* healed!"

It will be a happy day in the lives of many believers
when they realize that the God who loved us so much that
He gave His only begotten Son to die for us, will also
keep us and deliver us: "Being confident of this very
thing, that He which hath begun a good work in you will
perform it until the day of Jesus Christ" (Phil. 1:6).

Many believers are so occupied with trying to help
God get them through the Pearly Gates that they do not
have time to really enjoy the liberty of the grace of God.
They spend so much time fretting about whether or not
they will be able to "hold on and hold out" that they fail
to enjoy their spiritual birthright. Fellow believer, may
we realize that "by HIS stripes we are healed," and apart
from His stripes there IS no healing. There is nothing
that man can add to the finished work of Jesus. He bore
our sins, He settled the sin-question forever, and all that
WE can do is believe on Him and put our faith in His finished work. Jesus paid it all! Receive the gift of God—
and LIVE.

III.
The NEED of the Atonement

"*For ye were as sheep going astray.*"   Isaiah 53:6
tells us that "ALL we like sheep have gone astray."
Paul makes the same declaration in Romans 3:23: "ALL
have sinned, and come short of the glory of God." All
unregenerate souls are in the same sad state, spiritually.
What is said of Cain can be said of every sinner—"a fugitive

and a vagabond shalt thou be in the earth" (Gen. 4:12).

Isaiah 57:20,21 tells us, ". . . The wicked are like the troubled sea, when it cannot rest, whose waters cast up mire and dirt. *There is no peace, saith my God, to the wicked!*" Solomon said, ". . . The way of transgressors is hard" (Prov. 13:15).

The Lord likens man unto sheep; *unbelievers* are "as sheep going astray." A sheep differs from all other animals in its habits. When one sheep wanders away from the fold, it is not its tendency to seek the fold and return of its own accord, but rather to pursue its wandering until it falls prey to an enemy or until it starves. It must be *sought and brought back* to the fold. Other animals — the horse, the cow, the dog — will find their way back to their accustomed habitat. In Isaiah 1:3 we read, "The ox knoweth his owner, and the ass his master's crib: but Israel doth not know, my people doth not consider." The Holy Spirit made no mistake when *sheep* were used as a type of sinners, wandering until brought into the fold by the Good Shepherd.

History testifies to the fact that men do not seek God — it is GOD who does the seeking. Between Eden and Calvary we have four thousand years of the history of man — but do we find that he at any time sought God? He did not! He wandered farther and farther from God. Jesus came to pay the sin-debt at the darkest hour of human history up to that time. For four hundred years God had not even *spoken* to man. In the silent years from Malachi to Matthew, God did not bother to send a prophet to warn wicked men.

There is a teaching abroad in the land today to the effect that the Church will convert the world, bring in the kingdom, and, through the preaching of the Gospel, righteousness will finally cover the earth. But what saith the Scriptures? Does the Bible teach that the Church will convert the world and bring in the kingdom? If it does, let us preach it. If it does not, then let us declare what the Bible DOES teach about these days in which we live!

If we would know the answers to Bible questions, we must find those answers IN the Bible. In Matthew 13:24—30 Jesus clearly taught that the tares and the wheat would grow together until the end. In II Timothy 3:1—13 Paul clearly outlines the end-days as days of peril, sin, shame, and degradation; evil men and seducers will wax worse and worse, and all who live godly lives will suffer severe persecution. II Peter 3:10 clearly declares that the earth and all its works will be burned up and the elements shall melt with fervent heat.

Nowhere in the New Testament is it even suggested that the Church will convert the world. It was not *put* here to convert the world, but to make disciples of all men; and as it was in the days of Noah, as it was in the days of Lot, so shall it be when Jesus returns — first *for* His Church, and later WITH the Church to reign for a thousand glorious years here upon this earth. THEN — and ONLY then — will there be peace on earth, good will toward men. THEN the knowledge of the Lord will cover the earth as the waters now cover the sea.

If you will lift up your eyes and look upon the fields you will see that they are white unto harvest, and the laborers are so very few! It is easy to see that the whole world "lieth in wickedness" (or "in the lap of the wicked one") and the minority live lives of righteousness and holiness while the majority, like sheep, are going astray.

One reason for the tremendous increase in sin and the abundant fruits of sin is lack of pure Gospel preaching

66

in the pulpits of the world. The Gospel of the grace of God—the atonement, the shed blood—has been replaced by a social gospel. Liberalism and modernism have replaced fundamental Bible teaching in all too many pulpits.

But Jeremiah asks, "Can the Ethiopian change his skin, or the leopard his spots? Then may ye also do good, that are accustomed to do evil" (Jer. 13:23). As it was in the days of Jeremiah, so it is today. God's Word is still true:

"Ye must be born again" (John 3:7).

"Except ye repent, ye shall all likewise perish" (Luke 13:3,5).

"Boast not thyself of to morrow; for thou knowest not what a day may bring forth" (Prov. 27:1).

". . . Behold, now is the accepted time; behold, now is the day of salvation" (II Cor. 6:2).

"Today if ye will hear His voice, harden not your hearts" (Heb. 4:7).

IV.
The RESULTS of the Atonement

". . . *But are now returned unto the Shepherd and Bishop of your souls.*" The entire epistle of II Peter is directed to born again believers. Peter is speaking here of those who have believed on Christ unto salvation, having put their faith in His shed blood, thus having been regenerated by His Spirit. These are now "returned."

In the natural realm, when we refer to someone having *returned* to some particular place, we immediately think in terms of that person having been there before. Since Peter declares that we are returned to the Shepherd and Bishop of our *souls*, what is the meaning as having to do with hell-deserving sinners?

67

It seems the only possible meaning could be that through the vicarious suffering and the substitutionary death of Jesus, the believer is returned to fellowship such as Adam and Eve possessed in the Garden before they fell. Before sin entered Eden, Adam and Eve had fellowship with God personally, day by day; but when they sinned, that fellowship was broken.

The blood shed from Eden to Calvary only placed a shadow between God and the sinner; it could never take away sin. Please study Hebrews 10. The blood of animals simply put a shadow between the holiness of God and the sin of the sinner until the perfect Lamb should satisfy the holiness and the law of God through ONE sacrifice—the sacrifice of Himself and of His own blood. Therefore, through the atonement, man is returned to the fellowship he had with God before he sinned.

The relationship between God and the believer is even more desirable, more complete, than the fellowship Adam and Eve enjoyed in the Garden, because in Eden God said, "If you do what I told you NOT to do, you will die. If you break my commandment, you will die." But OUR relationship is not based on what we do or leave undone, from the standpoint of our relationship with God the Father, because JESUS satisfied the Father and we are IN Jesus now. Our relationship with God is determined by our standing in Jesus by faith. Righteousness has been imputed to us by faith, and God sees us righteous in Christ. We do not finally reach heaven by being able to abstain from certain things. *We reach heaven because we are IN CHRIST JESUS.* He said, "No man cometh unto the Father but by ME!"

Through the atoning blood we are returned to our Shepherd — the Good Shepherd who gave His life for the

68

sheep. A shepherd not only searches for the lost sheep until he finds it and brings it back into the fold; but he also tends the sheep. He feeds the flock and leads it into green pastures beside still waters. He restores the sheep when wounded, protects when in danger, defends the flock when enemies attack. The shepherd loves his sheep, and his goodness toward the flock never fails.

Our Lord Jesus Christ, our Good Shepherd, purchased all this and more in the atonement. In Him we find our every need supplied. He is our sufficiency, in Him we are complete.

In the atonement we find salvation from the *penalty* of sin, salvation from the *power* of sin, and the assurance that when He comes for His own, our Lord and Saviour will deliver us from the very *presence* of sin. He supplies our every need—physical, spiritual, mental, temporal, and eternal.

Have YOU trusted Jesus? If you have not, do it now! Bow your head and ask God to save you for Christ's sake — and He will save your soul. It was Jesus "who His own self bare our sins in His own body on the tree," that we, being dead to sin, should live unto righteousness. By His stripes we were healed.

"The Lord is my shepherd; I shall not want. He maketh me to lie down in green pastures: He leadeth me beside the still waters. He restoreth my soul: He leadeth me in the paths of righteousness for His name's sake. Yea, though I walk through the valley of the shadow of death, I will fear no evil: for thou art with me; thy rod and thy staff they comfort me. Thou preparest a table before me in the presence of mine enemies: thou anointest my head with oil; my cup runneth over. Surely goodness and mercy shall follow me all the days of my life: and I will dwell in the house of the Lord for ever" (Psalm 23).

If you know the first five words of this Psalm by heart (BY HEART, not from memory), then all the promises in the Psalm belong to you!

GOD'S GREAT FORGETTER

GOD'S GREAT FORGETTER

"For I will be merciful to their unrighteousness, and their sins and their iniquities will I remember no more" (Heb. 8:12).

"And their sins and iniquities will I remember no more" (Heb. 10:17).

Only a fool would deny the fact of sin. The evidence of sin is all around us. All one need do is open his eyes and *look*. We see the results of sin all around us. Every heartache, every heartbreak, every tear, every sorrow, every graveyard, every hospital is a testimony that *"the wages of sin is death."*

Sin is a dark cloud; but thank God, there is a rainbow of promise in "the Lamb of God who taketh away the sin of the world." "As in Adam *all die*, even so *in CHRIST shall all be made ALIVE"* (I Cor. 15:22).

Again . . . only a fool would deny the existence of God: "The fool hath said in his heart, There is no God" (Psa. 14:1). All one need do is stop, look, and listen. Any thinking person must admit there is a God. God has given everything a tongue with which to speak, to warn, to cry out. When we look at the sunrise in the morning, it speaks of "the Sun of Righteousness . . . with healing in His wings" (Mal. 4:2).

When we lift our eyes to heaven and see the stars twinkling in the sky, we are reminded of the Star of Bethlehem as it stood over the place where the baby Jesus lay . . . "For unto you is born this day in the city of David a Saviour, which is Christ the Lord" (Luke 2:11). When the soft winds blow, they whisper to us of the work of the

Holy Spirit. Jesus said to Nicodemus, "The wind bloweth where it listeth, and thou hearest the sound thereof, but canst not tell whence it cometh, and whither it goeth: so is every one that is born of the Spirit" (John 3:8).

When the darkness of night falls around us, the dark shadows prophesy of the "blackness of darkness forever," reserved for all the wicked at the end of a life of sin (Jude 13). The very home in which we dwell reminds us that Jesus said, "In my Father's house are many mansions . . . I go to prepare a place for you" (John 14:2).

Every time we approach a door we are reminded that Jesus is the Door to heaven: "I am the door: by me if any man enter in, he shall be saved, and shall go in and out, and find pasture" (John 10:9). "Behold, I stand at the door, and knock: if any man hear my voice, and open the door, I will come in to him, and will sup with him, and he with me" (Rev. 3:20).

When we sit down at the table at mealtime, the bread we eat testifies to us that Jesus is the Bread of Life (John 6:48). The cool water we drink reminds us that Jesus said to a poor, weary soul, "The water that I give . . . shall be . . . a well of water springing up into everlasting life" (John 4:14).

When we dress in the morning, our clothes remind us of the *robe of righteousness* which is ours for the receiving, through faith in the Lord Jesus. When we step into the great outdoors and behold the beautiful flowers, we think of Jesus, the "Lily of the Valley," the "Rose of Sharon." Every time we hear a little bird twitter in the trees above us, we are reminded that the heavenly Father sees every little sparrow—and not one of them shall fall to the ground unnoticed by Him.

When we drive through the countryside in the evening

74

and see the sheep coming into the fold, we remember that Jesus is our Good Shepherd, and "He careth for His sheep." When we see the little lambs, we think of Jesus, the Lamb of God. John said, "Behold the Lamb of God, which taketh away the sin of the world" (John 1:29).

We hear the crack of thunder, we see the flash of lightning—and the raindrops that begin to fall remind us of the terrible flood that God sent upon the wicked in Noah's day. Then, when the thunder has ceased to roll, the wind has calmed, and the raindrops have ceased to fall, the bright sun begins to shine—and a beautiful rainbow spans the horizon, reminding us of the promise of God unto all mankind.

Thus, while the evidence of sin is all around us, all creation speaks to us of Almighty God, our Creator, and of His Son, who came into this world and gave His life to *"take away the sin of the world"*! The sin each of us inherited from Adam cannot be denied; and those of us who believe the Bible do not desire to deny that Jesus paid the penalty for all sin. If we exercise faith in His finished work, then all sin is atoned for through His shed blood, and through Him we have life. The last Adam (the Lord Jesus Christ) bought back all that the first Adam lost by yielding to Satan. Were this not true, every baby born into this world would drop into the pit at death. The little innocent baby who dies goes to *heaven*, because the death it received from Adam is removed by the death of Christ.

No person can be lost because of Adam's sin. Men who die and go to hell do not go there because of Adam's sin—but *because they rejected the Lord Jesus Christ*. The innocent infant (in spite of what some religionists teach and preach) goes to paradise the split second it dies. Yes, infants who are not baptized according to the ritual of some religions also go to paradise at death. David said, after the death of his baby, "I shall go to him, but he shall not return to me." David believed (and declared under inspiration of the Holy Spirit) that his baby who died went to paradise at death, even though it was born in sin and born of a sinful union. Every little baby who dies before the age of accountability (and what that age is, no man knows) goes to be with the Lord in paradise.

In Christ we have the Light that "lighteth every man that cometh into the world" (John 1:9). Peter preached in Acts 5:30,31, "The God of our fathers raised up Jesus, whom ye slew and hanged on a tree. Him hath God exalted with His right hand to be a Prince and a Saviour, for to give repentance to Israel, *and forgiveness of sins.*" Again we read, ". . . Through this Man is preached unto you the *forgiveness of sins*" (Acts 13:38b). There is no other way, there is no other forgiveness, there is none who can forgive sins "save Jesus Christ only." Jesus is the propitiation for our sins—"and not for our's only, but also for the sins of the whole world" (I John 2:2).

Anyone desiring to know the whole Bible truth concerning God and the forgiveness of sins can find that truth in one verse: "For there is one God, and *one Mediator between God and men, the Man Christ Jesus*" (I Tim. 2:5). There is no other atonement. There is no other Mediator. "Neither is there salvation in any other: *for there is none other name under heaven given among men, whereby we must be saved*" (Acts 4:12).

What is *our* part in salvation? What must we do to be rid of sin? The only place to find the right answer is in the Word of God. In I John 1:9 we have this clear, understandable statement: "If we confess our sins, He is faithful and just to forgive us our sins, and to cleanse us from all unrighteousness."

That verse of Scripture is very easily understood. *Our part* is to confess our sins to the Lord Jesus (the only Mediator). He is faithful and just; He forgives us our sins, and He cleanses us from all unrighteousness. You may ask, "Brother Greene, how do I confess my sins to Jesus? Must I name my sins to my pastor or to my priest—or to the bishop?" No, indeed! The Bible does not command us to confess our sins to anyone on this earth. If you want a true prayer of confession, you will find one in Luke 18:13: ". . . God, be merciful to me a sinner!" The man who prayed that prayer went home justified — and to be justified is to stand before God just as though you had never committed a sin. Justification comes through the blood of Jesus — and when we are justified our sins are covered by the blood, and we stand before God as pure as the blood that covers us!

There is also a prayer of confession in Luke 23:42: ". . . Lord, remember me when Thou comest into Thy kingdom." In answer to that prayer, Jesus said to the penitent thief, "Today shalt thou be with me in paradise." If you sincerely pray a prayer of confession from your heart, God will forgive your sins and write your name in the Lamb's Book of Life—for Christ's sake (Eph. 4:32).

In I John 1:7 we read, ". . . The blood of Jesus Christ (God's) Son cleanseth us from all sin." Sin pollutes the soul — and all that you can do will never take away that pollution nor take away the guilt. The only power known to God or man that will remove the pollution and the guilt of sin and cleanse the heart from *all* sin is the blood of Jesus Christ. Jesus is *"the righteousness of God."*

Another verse that will help exceedingly in understanding what we must do concerning the sin question is Titus 3:5: "Not by works of righteousness which we have done, but according to His mercy He saved us, by the washing of regeneration, and renewing of the Holy Ghost." Now what is our part in that verse of Scripture? Paul clearly states to Titus, "*Not by works of righteousness which we have done . . . .*" Paul believed that cleansing and forgiveness of sin come by the mercy of God—the gift of God through the blood of the Lord Jesus Christ—and not through anything that man can do with his own hands or of himself.

In Ephesians 2:8,9 we are told, "For by grace are ye saved through faith; and that not of yourselves: it is the gift of God: not of works, lest any man should boast." Religions that preach works—or grace *plus works*—are growing by leaps and bounds throughout the world. I read in the newspaper recently that one of the outstanding religions of this day claims 500,000,000 members — and last year it grew in numbers to a greater degree than all other religions combined! That particular religion offers to its people the right of confession to a man — and the assurance that this man will atone for their sins. *That is strictly contrary to the Word of God.* If we confess our sins to JESUS—*not to man*—Jesus forgives. *Man cannot forgive sins*! The only way *anyone* can receive forgiveness for sin is to believe in the finished work of the Lord Jesus, accept Him by faith, and trust Him as our Saviour.

Someone may be asking, "What does God DO with all of our sins?" Again, the only place to find the right answer is in the Word of God. Micah 7:19 tells us that *God casts our sins into the depths of the sea*: "He will turn again, He will have compassion upon us; He will subdue our iniquities; and thou wilt cast all their sins into the depths of the sea."

According to reports I have read, the sea is mighty

deep! I am so thankful that my sins are cast into the depths of the sea. My sins are covered OCEAN DEEP! I am glad God did not cover my sins in a shallow lake of water. A lake might go dry sometime, and my sins would be exposed. Or it might become turbulent and toss them to the top, where they would be washed ashore. But thank God — my sins are cast into the depths of the sea, never to be disturbed by the storms of life. They are cast into the *very depths of the deepest sea.* No wonder Paul said, "There is therefore now no condemnation to them which are in Christ Jesus!" (Rom. 8:1).

In Psalm 103:12 the Bible declares, *"As far as the east is from the west,* so far hath He removed our transgressions from us."

Beloved, have you ever thought about the fact that both the North Pole and the South Pole have been discovered and reached by man, but that no one has ever heard of the *"east pole"* nor of the *"west pole"*? The Bible is foolproof. It has no loopholes, it has no mistakes, no errors. If the Scripture had said, "Our sins are removed as far as the *north* is from the *south,"* then someone would have said, "The devil can surely find them at the North Pole or the South Pole—in cold storage!" Thank God, there IS no *east pole* nor *west pole* — and when the devil starts looking for my sins he will never find them. I rejoice in the Bible truth that my sins are gone "as far as the east is from the west."

Isaiah puts it this way: "I have blotted out, as a thick cloud, thy transgressions, and, as a cloud, thy sins" (Isa. 44:22). Ezekiel 18:22 adds this marvelous word of information concerning where our sins are and what God has done with them: "All his transgressions that he hath committed, they shall not be mentioned unto him: in his righteousness that he hath done he shall live." Behold— no words can describe the truth of that verse of Scripture! Think of it! Transgressions committed by us, when covered by the precious blood of Jesus, shall never be mentioned to us again. They are covered, never to be brought up. Thank God for such a covering for our sins.

When a criminal is pardoned in the courts of our land, his past crime is often brought up by those who know him. We sometimes say, "His crime will follow him to his grave." The state and the law of the land may completely pardon him—but his enemies will never forget the crime he committed; and though his friends may never question it, they, too, will remember.

But God is not like that. God will never mention nor remember our sins. He will never throw them in our face; they are gone forever in the depths of the sea—blotted out as a thick cloud, never to be remembered against us. Thank God, there is NO condemnation to them that are in Christ Jesus.

Let us look at the words of our text: ". . . *their sins and iniquities will I remember no more.*" Beloved, these words could be true of none other than Almighty God. When our friends let us down or commit some wrong against us, we may forgive them sincerely and wholeheartedly—but we never forget it . . . we *cannot* forget it. We may SAY we forgive and forget, but the mind of man can never completely erase the memory of a wrong committed against him. There may be no bitterness or resentment, there may be no remaining hurt—but the memory is there.

But *God is not man.* God *completely forgets.* When I was a sinner, I was a *very wicked* sinner. I still remember many ugly things that I did in those days. Sometimes they cross my mind and I am reminded of them. I regret them.

I am not proud of my former ungodliness, but many times I mention it in my sermons as an illustration of what God can do for a poor, wicked sinner. It is utterly impossible for ME to forget the things I did before I was saved . . . I wish I *could* forget . . . but what rejoices my heart is the fact that GOD has *completely forgotten my sins*! He remembers them against me no more. He will never bring them up to be used against me. How wonderful to know that all of our past wickedness is gone forever!

"What shall we then say to these things? If God be for us, who can be against us? He that spared not His own Son, but delivered Him up for us all, how shall He not with Him also freely give us all things? Who shall lay anything to the charge of God's elect? It is God that justifieth. Who is he that condemneth? It is Christ that died, yea rather, that is risen again, who is even at the right hand of God, who also maketh intercession for us" (Rom. 8:31–34).

Such words could be spoken only by inspiration of the Holy Spirit. Such truth could be declared only by Almighty God, the Author of truth, and could be backed up by none other than He who said, "I AM the truth" (John 14:6).

Beloved, when we are saved by the grace of God, covered by the blood of Jesus, redeemed through His purchase price, there is absolutely nothing that can be brought against us because we are *in Christ Jesus*. Therefore the writer cries out, "Who can lay anything to the charge of God's elect?" Those who are born again He "did predestinate to be conformed to the image of His Son" (Rom. 8:29). These words are to be applied to those of us who *believe*, who have *received the Lord Jesus Christ* as our personal Saviour. Hallelujah! WHAT a Saviour!

Some of you may be thinking, "Preacher, I can go

along with you thus far. I do believe my sins are under the blood, that God has blotted them out as a thick cloud, that He has cast them into the depths of the sea and will remember them against me no more. But — what about the temptations that I will face today, tomorrow . . . in the future?"

That is a timely question. I am glad that our "Great Forgetter" has not forgotten to take care of that. Temptation is not a sin . . . please note, I said *temptation* is not a sin. "Blessed is the man that endureth temptation: for when he is tried, he shall receive the crown of life, which the Lord hath promised to them that love Him" (James 1:12). According to that verse of Scripture, the man who is tempted is a happy man when he *endures* the temptations — because at the end of a life that endures temptation and overcomes by the grace of God and the blood of Jesus, that man will receive a crown of life. Someone has very aptly said, "We cannot keep the birds from flying over our heads, but we can keep them from building nests in our hair." God has taken care of the temptation problem. Let me give you a few Scriptures to help you see just what God has done concerning temptation:

God will (if it is best for us) keep us from being tempted . . . yes, God can keep us from even *being* tempted: "*I also will keep thee from the hour of temptation*" (Rev. 3:10). I know that the fundamental truth of this particular verse of Scripture applies primarily to the hour of great tribulation that will come upon the whole world, and has to do with the Church being kept from the hour of temptation. (The Church will go through no part of the Great Tribulation.) But God will keep *us* from temptation if He knows that the temptation is more than we can bear. God is able and willing, if in faith we ask Him to deliver us from being tempted.

82

If God *allows* us to fall into temptation, we should remember that "The Lord knoweth how to deliver the godly OUT of temptations, and to reserve the unjust unto the day of judgment to be punished" (II Pet. 2:9).

If we believe the Bible, we believe that God is omnipotent, omniscient—and *omnipresent* . . . He is everywhere. He sees all, and He knows the end from the beginning. Therefore, if God loved us so much that He gave Jesus to die for us to keep us out of hell, certainly His love does not stop when He sees one of His children being put to a test by the devil. Yes, God can keep us *from* the hour of temptation—but if we *fall* into temptation He is able to deliver us: "There hath no temptation taken you but such as is common to man: but God is faithful, who will not suffer you to be tempted above that ye are able; but will with the temptation also make a way to escape, that ye may be able to bear it" (I Cor. 10:13). If you are a child of God and you do not know that Scripture from memory, I beg you to memorize that verse NOW. Do not take one more step in your Christian experience until you have committed it to memory.

Let me use just a few moments to analyze this important verse for you:

"There hath no temptation taken YOU (*the verse is very personal; YOU are the one to whom this great truth is directed*) but such as is common to man . . . ." You may think that you have more to put up with than anyone else on this earth. You may think that you have been put to the test as no other has ever been tested. But dear friend, read those words again: ". . . *but such as is common to man.*" Every temptation *you* have ever had has also been hurled across the paths of other Christians.

There are three avenues through which the devil works:

"*the lust of the flesh, and the lust of the eyes, and the pride of life*" (I John 2:15–17). When Satan tempted Jesus as recorded in Matthew 4:1–12, he used all three of these avenues of temptation — but Jesus conquered them all and put the devil to flight. Paul tells us that Jesus was tempted in all points as we are, "yet without sin" (Heb. 4:15).

"There hath no temptation taken you but such as is common to man — BUT GOD IS FAITHFUL . . . ." Hallelujah! GOD is faithful! Dear friend, even though YOU may fail, God Almighty CANNOT prove unfaithful. When God has promised, He will keep His promise. *God IS faithful!* Read on: ". . . who will not suffer you to be tempted (*God will not allow the devil to tempt you*) above that ye are able . . . ." There is the personal message again: "*above that YE are able.*" God will not allow the devil to put more on you than you are able to bear.

Now hear these precious words: ". . . but will with the temptation also make a way to escape, *that ye may be able to bear it*"! In *God's faithfulness* He will not allow the devil to put more on you than you are able to bear, "but will with the temptation make a way to escape, that YOU may be able to bear it"!

Let me repeat: If you do not know that verse from memory, hide it in your mind and heart this moment. Do not live another day of your Christian life without memorizing that verse of Scripture.

You see, dear brothers and sisters in Christ, we are not serving a God who cannot be touched with the feeling of our infirmities. We are not serving a great, gigantic, spiritual being somewhere far beyond the blue, sitting on a throne in some remote section of outer space. You and I as believers are serving a God and following a Christ

84

who sympathizes with all who are tempted: "He Himself hath suffered being tempted" (Heb. 2:18). Jesus not only suffered on the cross, He also suffered through every avenue of temptation the devil knows. Yes, Jesus was sinless — but you must remember *He was the God-Man*. He was God — and yet He was man; and He suffered in the same identical way that you and I suffer when put to severe temptation by the devil.

You may say, "Brother Greene, do you mean to tell me that Jesus was put to every test that I have been put to?" No, *I* do not mean to tell you that; I will let the *Scripture* tell you: "(Jesus) was in all points tempted like as we are, yet without sin" (Heb. 4:15). If you believe the Bible, you must believe that Jesus was tested, tempted, and tried in every point that you and I have ever suffered in temptation. When we are tempted, we are not to drop our head and act as though God is dead and we have lost everything. Listen to these precious words: "My brethren, count it all joy when ye fall into divers temptations: knowing this, that the trying of your faith worketh patience" (James 1:2,3).

When a person tells you that he is never tempted, that he never suffers persecution for the sake of Jesus Christ, mark it down that he is a child of the devil! Christians are tempted — and WILL BE tempted as long as we remain in this body of flesh. Again I quote, *"Blessed is the man that endureth temptation."* Instead of being despondent and discouraged, we should thank God for the joy of being tempted and overcoming temptation *in Him!* Yes, in Christ Jesus we are "more than conquerors" (Rom. 8:35–39).

Let me close this message with another marvelous Gospel truth: "Let your conversation be without covetousness; and be content with such things as ye have: for He hath said, *I will never leave thee, nor forsake thee.* So that we may boldly say, The Lord is my helper, and I will not fear what man shall do unto me" (Heb. 13:5,6).

And now, let us sum up what we have learned from God's Word in studying this message:

First of all, we found that the Bible teaches that in Adam all die—but in Christ all are made alive, thank God. What Adam lost by disobedience, Jesus purchased (bought back) with His perfect obedience—obedience even unto the death on the cross. Sin as a dark cloud separates us from God; but if we confess our sins, God removes them as far as the east is from the west. He cleanses us from all iniquity and covers our sins ocean-deep. He puts them behind His back; He blots them out. Not one time will He mention them against us.

In the second place, we learned that just as truly as God has taken care of the sin question BEHIND us, He also takes care of the sin question BEFORE us in the days that we remain upon this earth. God can keep us from temptation — but if we fall into temptation, God is able to deliver us. Jesus sympathizes with those who are tempted, because HE was tempted in all points as we are—and yet He never sinned. Therefore, *He is able to give us the victory over temptation.* Believers should rejoice when tempted, knowing that we are more than conquerors through Him that loved us. We should count it a joy to be put to the test for the glory of God.

Last—but by no means least—we have that glorious promise: "I will never leave thee, nor forsake thee." Let me say "Amen" by quoting for you one of the most precious verses in all of God's Word: "For He hath made Him to be sin for us, who knew no sin; that we might be made the righteousness of God in Him" (II Cor. 5:21).

SALVATION AND VICTORY

SALVATION AND VICTORY

The devil has had six thousand years' experience in deception. He is the master deceiver, the father of liars. His first desire concerning every person on earth is to damn that person to the lowest hell; but if the sinner repents and trusts Jesus for remission of sin, thereby becoming a child of God, *then* Satan immediately begins a campaign to wreck the joy and destroy the testimony of that person whose soul he lost to the grace of God.

To the sinner, the devil advances this argument: "Salvation is not for you. The Gospel and religion are all right for old folk, sick folk, and children—but not for YOU. And even if you did get saved you could not live the Christian life; you would only stay with it for a little while. Think of your job, your background, your family — and what would your friends and neighbors think? It simply is not meant for YOU to live a Christian life; there are too many obstacles in your way. Why not just forget all about it?"

Satan uses every means at his command to prevent the sinner's being saved. Recently I talked with a young man who told me that he had almost lost his mind in his search for salvation. He went to revivals, he went forward for prayer, he bowed at the altar and prayed, confessed his sins, and begged for salvation—but gave up in despair. Why? Because he could not meet the requirements of the ministers who dealt with him!

According to *their* blueprint for salvation, that young man could not be saved. But thanks be to God, someone gave him a simple, understandable Gospel tract that contained the plan of salvation *according to GOD'S blueprint of salvation by grace through faith*—"the gift of God, not of works, lest any man should boast" (Eph. 2:8,9); and in the quietness of his own home the young man sat down, read the tract, saw the truth of how God, by His grace and according to His mercy, saves us by the regeneration of the power of the shed blood and the Holy Spirit. He accepted Jesus and was gloriously saved. He is now a happy, victorious Christian.

He said to me, "Brother Greene, God saved me in spite of preachers and religious fanatics who demanded that I act exactly as *they* did when *they* were saved. I am saved *in spite* of them, not *because* of them. If it had been left up to them to win me to Jesus I would have gone to hell."

How sad! Saved in spite of preachers! If the devil can get a minister to add a little or subtract a little where the plan of salvation is concerned, if he can persuade him to supplement the Gospel with doctrines and creeds of men, that minister is the devil's best friend.

If YOU have tried to be saved and failed, the only reason you are not saved is because you tried to be saved *your* way or *man's* way and not GOD'S way. Perhaps you were seeking the same experience, the same reactions others had when *they* were saved. The only way to be saved is to put your trust in Jesus and ASK Him to save you. Then believe His promise, and on the basis of the Word of God acknowledge your salvation and thank Him for saving you!

What makes a person a sinner in the first place? The answer most often given to that question is, "I am a sinner because I drink, swear, steal, gamble, etc., etc. . . . I am going to hell because I am a drunkard." It is true that

90

those who *die* drunkards go to hell (I Cor. 6:10), but sinner friend, if you die and go to hell today, it will not be the sins you have *committed today* that will send you there. It will not be the liquor you drank today nor the cursing you did today that will damn you. It will be the sin of unbelief—your refusal to accept Christ as your Saviour.

Rejecting Jesus *just one time* is sufficient sin to damn a soul forever; but according to God's Word, each rejection of His invitation makes it easier to reject Him the next time. Paul speaks of those "having their conscience seared with a hot iron" (I Tim. 4:2).

The admonition in Hebrews 4:7 is, "TO DAY if ye will hear His voice, harden not your hearts!" And the warning in Proverbs 29:1 is, "He, that being often reproved hardeneth his neck, shall suddenly be destroyed, and that without remedy."

HERE IS THE BIBLE TRUTH

"He came unto His own, and His own received Him not" (John 1:11).

". . . He that believeth not is condemned already, because he hath not believed in the name of the only begotten Son of God" (John 3:18b).

". . . Ye will not come to me, that ye might have life" (John 5:40).

"How shall we escape, if we neglect so great salvation . . . ?" (Heb. 2:3).

". . . He that believeth not God hath made Him a liar; because he believeth not the record that God gave of His Son" (I John 5:10b).

Unbelief—rejecting Jesus, refusing to believe what God says in His precious Word—is to make Him a liar. To realize the need of a Saviour, to know according to the

91

Scriptures that Jesus died for the sins of the world, and yet to refuse to trust Him as Saviour is to stand condemned, *an enemy to God.* Jesus said, "He that is not with me is against me . . ." (Matt. 12:30).

ON THE OTHER HAND

". . . As many as *received Him,* to them gave He power to become the sons of God, even to them that believe on His name: which were born, not of blood, nor of the will of the flesh, nor of the will of man, but of God" (John 1:12,13).

"He that believeth on Him *is not condemned . . .*" (John 3:18a).

". . . He that heareth my Word, and believeth on Him that sent me, hath everlasting life, and shall not come into condemnation; but is passed from death unto life" (John 5:24).

". . . Him that cometh to me I will in no wise cast out" (John 6:37).

"Come unto me, all ye that labour and are heavy laden, and I will give you rest" (Matt. 11:28).

"Believe on the Lord Jesus Christ, and thou shalt be saved . . ." (Acts 16:31).

"Whosoever shall call upon the name of the Lord shall be saved" (Rom. 10:13).

"There is therefore now *no condemnation* to them which are in Christ Jesus . . ." (Rom. 8:1).

"For by grace are ye saved through faith; and that not of yourselves: it is the gift of God: Not of works, lest any man should boast" (Eph. 2:8,9).

"Not by works of righteousness which we have done, but according to His mercy He saved us, by the washing of regeneration, and renewing of the Holy Ghost" (Tit. 3:5).

REJECTING JESUS DAMNS—RECEIVING JESUS SAVES

One sin damns the sinner; *many* sins make hell worse for those who go there. The Bible clearly teaches that sinners will be judged and rewarded according to their wickedness. It is better never to hear the Gospel at all than to hear the plan of salvation, reject it, and go on in sin. Sins committed after hearing and rejecting the Gospel will make hell hotter for the sinner.

Jesus said, "That servant, which *knew* his lord's will, and prepared not himself, neither did according to his will, shall be beaten with *many* stripes. But he that knew not, and did commit things worthy of stripes, shall be beaten with *few* stripes" (Luke 12:47,48a).

II Peter 2:21 tells us, "It had been better for them not to have known the way of righteousness, than, after they have known it, to turn from the holy commandment delivered unto them."

John the Beloved tells us, "I saw the dead, small and great, stand before God; and the books were opened: and another book was opened, which is the book of life: and the dead were judged out of those things which were written in the books, ACCORDING TO THEIR WORKS" (Rev. 20:12). *"The dead"* here refers to sinners only. There will be no righteous dead at this judgment.

Sinners do not go to hell because they drink, curse, lie, steal, commit adultery, murder, etc. *They go to hell because they reject Jesus!*

WHAT ABOUT LIVING THE CHRISTIAN LIFE?

When a sinner comes to Christ for salvation, the devil knows he has lost the soul of that person, but he does not give up the battle — oh, no! The minute a sinner is saved, all hell declares war on the "babe in Christ." Remember,

Satan is "the accuser of the brethren" (Rev. 12:10), and to the new Christian he says:

"Now look what you did — and you claim to be saved! Would a Christian lose his temper? Would a Christian become discouraged or frustrated by circumstances? Would a Christian pray with so little faith? If you were *really* saved would God not have given you what you asked for?" And in a thousand ways the devil tries to prevail upon the babe in Christ to throw up his hands and say, "What's the use! I simply *cannot* live the Christian life."

But the Lord lovingly invites, "Come now, and let us reason together . . ." (Isa. 1:18). Dear friend, since Jesus loved you enough to die for you, is it not reasonable to believe that He is far more interested in your making a success in the Christian life than YOU are? He has a lot more invested in YOU than you do in HIM. He purchased your soul at the tremendous price of His precious blood. You are His purchased possession, and "*having loved His own which were in the world, He loved them unto the end*" (John 13:1b).

Jesus is a loving, understanding, compassionate, forgiving Saviour. He has promised, "I will never leave thee, nor forsake thee. So that we may boldly say, The Lord is my Helper, and I will not fear what man shall do unto me" (Heb. 13:5,6).

I John 2:1,2 tells us, "My little children, these things write I unto you, that ye sin not. And if any man sin, we have an Advocate with the Father, Jesus Christ the righteous: and He is the propitiation for our sins: and not for our's only, but also for the sins of the whole world."

Jesus made provision for all the blunders and shortcomings of His "little children." He does not want us to sin, but if we DO sin He does not turn His back on us and

94

disown us. He wants us to come to Him, confess our sins—and He is faithful to *forgive* and to cleanse us from all unrighteousness.

"The Lord is merciful and gracious, slow to anger, and plenteous in mercy. . . He hath not dealt with us after our sins; nor rewarded us according to our iniquities. For as the heaven is high above the earth, so great is His mercy toward them that fear Him. As far as the east is from the west, so far hath He removed our transgressions from us. Like as a father pitieth his children, so the Lord pitieth them that fear Him. For He knoweth our frame; He remembereth that we are dust" (Psalm 103:8–14).

Young Christian friend, you who are new in the Christian life, is the devil telling YOU that you cannot live the faith you profess? Is he telling you that you are weak and that you might as well give up and quit? If so, REJOICE! That is a good sign that you are sàved and that you are going to amount to something in your Christian experience. The devil would not be so worried about you if you were NOT saved, because you would still be his property, under his control. The very fact that he is trying so hard to discourage you is a good sign that you CAN make good and be a strong testimony for Jesus.

James 4:7 tells us, "Submit yourselves therefore to God. *Resist the devil, and he will flee from you.*"

Beloved, JESUS has already won the victory for you! All you have to do is claim it in His name. Listen: "Whosoever is born of God overcometh the world: and this is the victory that overcometh the world, even our faith" (I John 5:4).

I John 4:4 assures us, "*Ye are of GOD*, little children, and have overcome them: because *greater is He (Jesus) that is in you*, than he (Satan) that is in the world!" ·

When the devil comes to you with discouragement in your Christian life, remind him in the words of Paul:

"If God be FOR us, who can be against us? . . . Who shall lay anything to the charge of God's elect? It is God that justifieth. Who is he that condemneth? It is Christ that died, yea, rather, that is risen again, *who is even at the right hand of God, who also maketh intercession for us.* . . . We are MORE than conquerors through Him that loved us. For I am persuaded, that neither death, nor life, nor angels, nor principalities, nor powers, nor things present, nor things to come, nor height, nor depth, nor any other creature, shall be able to separate us from the love of God, which is in Christ Jesus our Lord!" (Rom. 8:31–39).

Jesus is not only the author of our salvation, He is also the *finisher* of our faith (Heb. 12:2). He saves us, He keeps us, and He will present us "faultless before the presence of His glory with exceeding joy" (Jude 24).

Our entering heaven depends upon the shed blood of Jesus and our faith IN His shed blood.

Our victory over the world, the flesh, and the devil depends upon our trusting Jesus day by day. Victory in the Christian life does not come through striving, enduring, or laboring. Victory comes through our faith in Christ's ability to do what He promised us He would do if we would trust Him.

Sinner friend, *GOD WANTS you to be saved*: "For God so loved the world, that He gave His only begotten Son, that *whosoever* believeth in Him should not perish, but have everlasting life" (John 3:16).

JESUS wants you to be saved: Matthew 20:28 tells us that He came into the world "not to be ministered unto, but to minister, *and to give His life a ransom for many.*"

96

The soul-saving message of the Gospel is that "Christ died for our sins according to the Scriptures; and that He was buried, and that He rose again the third day according to the Scriptures" (I Cor. 15:3,4).

God has done all in His power to keep you from spending eternity in hell. He is "not willing that ANY should perish, but that ALL should come to repentance" (II Pet. 3:9).

BUT THAT IS NOT ALL

The Holy Spirit is in the world to do all in *HIS* power to keep you out of hell! Jesus said, "When He (the Holy Spirit) is come, He will reprove the world of sin, and of righteousness, and of judgment" (John 16:8). The Holy Spirit reminds you of your sin, urges you to live right, plants in your bosom the fear of judgment at the hands of a righteous God. The Spirit knocks at the heart's door of each and every sinner (Rev. 3:20).

The eternal Godhead exhausted the riches of heaven to keep sinners out of hell! He wants you saved a million times worse than YOU WANT to be saved. He will save you if you will only commit yourself to Him in Jesus' name.

If you are saying, "I know God can save me—but I am afraid I cannot live the Christian life AFTER I am saved," then let me ask you, *"Who told you that?"* It had to be the devil or one of his puppets in the pulpit! *God* did not tell you any such thing; and you may rest assured that any thought you may have along that line came from the devil— not from Jesus nor from the Holy Spirit.

The Christian can say with confidence, *"The Lord is MY Shepherd. . . He leadeth me in the paths of right living for His name's sake."* The Holy Spirit DOES lead the child of God in paths of righteousness—not that we might have something to brag about, but that we not bring dis-

97

grace upon His name.

You to whom Satan has said, "You cannot live a Christian life," should turn to I Corinthians 10:13 and commit that verse to memory:

"There hath no temptation taken you but such as is common to man: but GOD IS FAITHFUL, who will not suffer you to be tempted above that ye are able; but will with the temptation also make a way to escape, that ye may be able to bear it!"

What a promise! And if the devil has told you that it is impossible for you to live a Christian life, *what a liar he is!*

Friend, if you are not saved, bow your head and trust Jesus this moment. Confess to Him that you are lost, ask Him to save you — and He will!

If you are a *defeated Christian*, bow your head and trust Jesus for victory! The battle is the Lord's. OUR part is to "have faith in God" (Mark 11:22). God is ready, He is willing, He is able. Are YOU ready to trust your all to Him?

FOUR THINGS GOD CANNOT DO

FOUR THINGS GOD CANNOT DO

"Lord, thou hast been our dwelling place in all generations. Before the mountains were brought forth, or ever thou hadst formed the earth and the world, even from everlasting to everlasting, thou art God. . . The Lord He is God; there is none else beside Him" (Ps. 90:1,2; Deut. 4:35).

In the light of these verses, the subject of this message may sound a bit unscriptural. There are many false gods, but there is only ONE true and living God—omniscient, omnipresent, omnipotent. He holds all power in His mighty hands — and yet, there are four things God cannot do, *simply because He IS GOD.*

1. God cannot die:

". . . From everlasting to everlasting, thou art God." How long *is* "everlasting"? There are no measurements or calculations of time whereby man can answer that question. The finite mind cannot conceive the meaning of *everlasting.* The never-ending existence of our God is something we will never understand in this world.

Isaiah tells us, "My thoughts are not your thoughts, neither are your ways my ways, saith the Lord. For as the heavens are higher than the earth, so are my ways higher than your ways, and my thoughts than your thoughts" (Isa. 55:8,9).

Job tells us that God "doeth great things past finding out; yea, and wonders without number" (Job 9:10).

Look up — look as far as your eyes can see toward heaven. You can see the sun (which the scientists tell us is 93,000,000 miles away); we can see the stars (some of which, according to science, are farther away than the sun); and yet, God's Word tells us that *God's ways and thoughts* are just that much higher than *our* ways and our thoughts. That is the reason the finite mind cannot understand the everlasting eternity through which God will live.

God's calendar and timeclock do not travel in accordance with our estimation of time. Man deals in years; God deals in centuries. Peter tells us that "one day is with the Lord as a thousand years, and a thousand years as one day" (II Pet. 3:8).

Our Scripture says that God is FROM everlasting TO everlasting. That means that God has *always been*, He has always been GOD, and He will *continue to be God through the everlasting ages of eternity ahead.*

You may say, "Preacher, I do not understand that." We are not supposed to understand it, my friend. We are to take it by faith—"the substance of things hoped for, the evidence of things not seen" (Heb. 11:1). In this day men are saved and kept by the faith which comes by hearing the Word of God. And the Word of God tells us that God cannot die; He is from everlasting to everlasting.

Our loved ones must die, if Jesus tarries. Death will take our best friends from us, if Jesus tarries. Sometimes we are called upon to stand by the open grave of the one dearest to our hearts — and Paul tells us that *death* will be the last enemy to be destroyed (I Cor. 15:26). But praise God, death cannot rob us of our God, for He has power over death, hell, and the grave. Before the mountains were, He was! And when the mountains have been moved out of their places, when "the heavens shall pass away with a great noise, and the elements shall melt with fervent heat, the earth also and the works that are therein shall be burned up" (II Pet. 3:10), our God will still be, and He will still be GOD! *He cannot die.*

That is the reason that we who know God as our Father and Christ as our Saviour can boast of everlasting life. *We are born of an everlasting Father, we have become His everlasting children.* Our earthly life will pass unless Jesus comes for His own during our natural lifetime; but praise God, we who are born of the Spirit have *everlasting life* because our Father in heaven is from everlasting to everlasting!

2. God cannot lie:

". . . God, willing more abundantly to shew unto the heirs of promise the immutability of His counsel, confirmed it by an oath: that by two immutable things, *in which it was impossible for God to lie*, we might have a strong consolation, who have fled for refuge to lay hold upon the hope set before us" (Heb. 6:17,18).

". . . In hope of eternal life, which *God, that cannot lie*, promised before the world began" (Tit. 1:2).

Thank God, we have the promise of eternal life from One who cannot lie. We are living in a day when men think very little about lying; it bothers them not at all. They have even lied about the Word of God, twisting it to prove their own points of religion or their denominational beliefs.

But our God cannot lie — and that is why Paul tells us in Romans 3:4, "Let God be true, but every man a liar!" I often receive letters from people in radioland, asking me who (and what) to believe. If these dear folk will read their Bibles they will KNOW what to believe, for God cannot lie. I confess that books put out by the liberals and modernists—and even by the denominational bosses—are confusing; but THE Book, dictated by the Holy Spirit and penned down by holy men of old, will *eliminate confusion!*

Paul said with confidence, "I KNOW WHOM I HAVE BELIEVED . . ." (II Tim. 1:12). If we know WHOM we have believed, then we will as a matter of course know WHAT to believe.

I confess that this old world is in a terrible state of confusion insofar as religion is concerned. New sects are springing up almost every day, and others are changing their doctrines and programs. But the Blessed Book and its Author remain the same: "Jesus Christ the same yesterday, and to day, and for ever" (Heb. 13:8). *"Religion"* will confuse you—but God's Word promises, "Behold, I lay in Sion a chief corner stone, elect, precious: *and he that believeth on HIM shall not be confounded"* (I Pet. 2:6). Heaven and earth will pass away, but God's Word will never fail (Matt. 24:35).

Christians are not tossed about by every wind of doctrine; they do not change their religion every time a new preacher comes to town. I talked with a man the other day who told me that he had been a Catholic for several years, and then he became a Presbyterian and served as a deacon for several years. He then realized that he was keeping the wrong day of the week for worship, so he became a Seventh Day Adventist! It stands to reason that the next crowd that comes along with something he likes will be the crowd he will join. It really would not make any difference, because it doesn't hurt an empty bottle to change the label on it!

I am a Missionary Baptist, but I do not magnify the Baptist denomination. I am doing my best to magnify Christ. I thank God for my church, I thank Him for what the Church has done for men in the past; but I shall never cease to thank Him for JESUS, the One who bought my redemption with His own precious blood.

God, who cannot lie, holds out to us these promises: "Come unto me, all ye that labour and are heavy laden,

104

and I will give you rest" (Matt. 11:28).

". . . Jesus said unto them, I am the bread of life: he that cometh to me shall never hunger; and he that believeth on me shall never thirst . . . and him that cometh to me I will in no wise cast out" (John 6:35,37).

"Verily, verily, I say unto you, He that heareth my Word, and believeth on Him that sent me, hath everlasting life, and shall not come into condemnation; but is passed from death unto life" (John 5:24).

"For God so loved the world, that He gave His only begotten Son, that whosoever believeth in Him should not perish, but have everlasting life. . . He that believeth on Him is not condemned: but he that believeth not is condemned already, because he hath not believed in the name of the only begotten Son of God" (John 3:16,18).

Thank God, we can depend on every statement and promise that fell from the lips of the Lord Jesus! Many times when I am reading and studying the Word of God, I discover a new promise to the saved ones — and I confidently stand upon that promise, taking it as my very own. God cannot lie, and I know His promises are sure.

3.   God cannot see our sins through the blood of Jesus:

"And almost all things are by the law purged with blood; and without shedding of blood is no remission" (Heb. 9:22).

Blood was first shed to cover sin in the Garden of Eden when Adam and Eve deliberately disobeyed God and ate the fruit of the tree of the knowledge of good and evil— fruit they had been forbidden to eat. Immediately their eyes were opened, and they saw the shame of their nakedness. In an attempt to cover their disobedience and their shame they made aprons of fig leaves — but when God came walking in the garden in the cool of the day, they found that their covering was totally inadequate and they "hid themselves from the presence of the Lord God amongst the trees of the garden."

It is a familiar story, known since the beginning of the human race. God slew innocent animals and took their coats to make coverings for Adam and Eve. From that time forward, blood has been the price of sin's covering. And even in this day of bloodless preaching God still requires blood—*the blood of Jesus*—to cover sin!

Cain's offering of his fruit of the ground was rejected by God. Abel's offering of "the firstling of his flocks" was accepted because it was a blood offering. God deals in blood — if you accept the blood of Jesus, you *live* eternally. If you reject the blood of Jesus you *die* eternally. God's decree has not changed since that night in Egypt when He said to the Hebrews, *"When I see the BLOOD, I will pass over you"* (Ex. 12:13).

The death angel swept through Egypt that night and slew the firstborn in every house where he did not find blood on the door post. He did not knock at the door and ask if an Israelite lived there; he followed the directions of the Lord. And when you and I stand before the righteous Judge it will be the same story: "When I see the blood, I will pass over you!" Those who are not covered by the blood of Jesus will hear Him say, "Depart—I never knew you!"

He will not ask, "Did you teach in Sunday school? Did you work in the church?" He will not be interested in whether you were a preacher, a deacon, a steward, a singer in the church choir. Those who enter heaven will enter *through the blood*. There is no other way.

In Matthew 7:21–23 Jesus said, "Not every one that

106

saith unto me, Lord, Lord, shall enter into the kingdom of heaven; but he that doeth the will of my Father which is in heaven. Many will say to me in that day, Lord, Lord, have we not prophesied in thy name? and in thy name have cast out devils? and in thy name done many wonderful works? And then will I profess unto them, *I NEVER KNEW YOU: Depart from me, ye that work iniquity!*"

What is wrong with these folk? They have prophesied (preached) in the name of Jesus, they have cast out devils, they have done many wonderful works. Why are they to be denied entrance into the kingdom of God? *They are not under the BLOOD*, my friend. Blood is not mentioned one time in the accomplishments of these people. One may work diligently, serve faithfully, live morally above reproach, and give sacrificially of his earthly store — but if that is all he has to offer, he is lost. It takes BLOOD to cover sin!

But thanks be unto God, when we accept Jesus as our Saviour and come under the cleansing power of His blood, God cannot see our sins. He sees us "in the Beloved," and "the blood of Jesus Christ His Son cleanseth us from all sin" (I John 1:7).

In Romans 5:8,9 Paul said, ". . . God commendeth His love toward us, in that, while we were yet sinners, Christ died for us. *Much more then, being now justified by His blood, we shall be saved from wrath through Him.*"

What does it mean to be *justified* in the sight of God? Someone has said that it means to be just as just as JESUS is just. We are justified by His blood, our sins are covered by His blood; and God cannot see our sins through the precious blood of Jesus.

4. God cannot save a soul unless that soul is willing to be saved:

107

If God could save a person against his will, then God would be a dictator and Christians would be slaves — but God is NOT a dictator. He is a loving Father, and man is a free moral agent.

God created man in His own image, breathed into his nostrils the breath of life, and man became a living soul. God put him in the Garden of Eden, gave him a helpmate, and placed at his disposal everything man's heart could desire. But in that garden He also put the tree of forbidden fruit.

God told Adam what he could eat, and what he was NOT to eat — and to that command he attached a penalty for disobedience: "Of the tree of the knowledge of good and evil, *thou shalt not eat of it*: for in the day that thou eatest thereof *thou shalt surely die*" (Gen. 2:17).

Thus, He made the Garden of Eden a garden of choice. Adam had everything that was beautiful to look upon and good for food. There was no excuse for His eating the forbidden fruit—but if God *had not* put the tree of the knowledge of good and evil within their reach, then Adam and Eve would have been God's slaves. They would have had no choice to make.

God does not *force* men to follow Him. His invitation has always been, "Come now, and let us reason together... Come unto me, and I will give you rest." God came to man in the Man Christ Jesus. Now it is up to man to come to God *through* Christ Jesus. But it must be the sinner's *choice* to receive eternal life; God cannot save him against his will!

The parable of the prodigal son bears out the truth that God could not save a sinner against his will and still be God. The father in the parable knew that the young son should not take his part of the inheritance and leave

108

home; but he allowed the son to make a choice. The boy took his share of the money and took HIS journey. If the father had done what he knew was best he would not have let the boy leave — but if he had confined him and kept him *from* going, the son would have been the father's prisoner or slave.

God knows what is best for us; but many times, instead of seeking His direction and following His advice, we do things and go places in the opposite direction from that in which He would lead us. Jesus refers to Himself as "the Good Shepherd," and a good shepherd *leads* his sheep, he does not drive them. God wants to be man's Shepherd, but there are so many who will not follow His leading—and *He does not drive us.*

We who know the Lord and His goodness should pray for Him to send down conviction upon this old world, to make men realize their need of a Saviour. It is when sinners realize their lost condition, when they realize that they are on the road to hell and can do nothing to save themselves, that they will call upon the Lord for mercy — and when sinners call for mercy, God is ready and anxious to save!

Jesus came into the world to give His life a ransom for sin. He is waiting, able, and anxious to save all who will come to Him; but if sinners refuse to come to Him, He cannot save them. He will not force men to be saved. He will not force them to serve Him.

If you are not a Christian, I plead with you to come to Jesus this moment and allow Him to come into your heart.

"Believe on the Lord Jesus Christ, and thou shalt be saved, and thy house" (Acts 16:31).

WOULD YOU PANIC OR WOULD YOU PRAY?

WOULD YOU PANIC OR WOULD YOU PRAY?

"It pleased Darius to set over the kingdom an hundred and twenty princes, which should be over the whole kingdom; and over these three presidents; of whom Daniel was first: that the princes might give accounts unto them, and the king should have no damage. Then this Daniel was preferred above the presidents and princes, because an excellent spirit was in him; and the king thought to set him over the whole realm.

"Then the presidents and princes sought to find occasion against Daniel concerning the kingdom; but they could find none occasion nor fault; forasmuch as he was faithful, neither was there any error or fault found in him. Then said these men, We shall not find any occasion against this Daniel, except we find it against him concerning the law of his God. Then these presidents and princes assembled together to the king, and said thus unto him, King Darius, live for ever. All the presidents of the kingdom, the governors, and the princes, the counsellors, and the captains, have consulted together to establish a royal statute, and to make a firm decree, that whosoever shall ask a petition of any God or man for thirty days, save of thee, O king, he shall be cast into the den of lions. Now, O king, establish the decree, and sign the writing, that it be not changed, according to the law of the Medes and Persians, which altereth not.

"Wherefore king Darius signed the writing and the decree. Now when Daniel knew that the writing was signed, he went into his house; and his windows being open in his chamber toward Jerusalem, he kneeled upon his knees three times a day, and prayed, and gave thanks before his God, as he did aforetime" (Daniel 6:1—10).

The book of Daniel has always been one of my favorite sources of study. It has stirred my heart many times. I have read it over, and over, and over again.

The devil has long sought to destroy this marvelous portion of the Word of God. He has attacked it through liberals and modernists, and many have declared that it should even be removed from the Holy Scriptures. But Jesus put *His* stamp of approval upon the book of Daniel when He declared, "When ye therefore shall see the abomination of desolation, *spoken of by Daniel the prophet*, stand in the holy place . . ." (Matt. 24:15); and since JESUS recognized Daniel as God's prophet, *you and I* had better recognize him as God's prophet. ". . . Let God be true, but every man a liar" (Rom. 3:4).

Daniel, a Hebrew captive in Babylon, had found favor with King Darius, and had been placed "above the presidents and princes, because an excellent spirit was in him; and the king thought to set him over the whole realm." Undoubtedly the king had recognized in Daniel a much greater man than he had supposed, and the position to which he appointed him was second in power only to that of the king himself.

This appointment brought real trouble to Daniel, for through jealousy and envy the presidents and princes "sought to find occasion against him." They could find no fault with him, however, in his relationship to the kingdom, for he was honest, loyal, faithful in all of his duties in the palace. They eventually came to the conclusion that the only way they could bring any charge against this man who stood so high in favor with the king, was to charge him through his relationship to Jehovah God.

Evidently they were well acquainted with Daniel's faith and devotion to God, and they knew that he would forfeit his life before he would renounce the one true God and turn his worship elsewhere.

Therefore they persuaded the king to sign a decree

that "whosoever shall ask a petition of any God or man for thirty days, save of thee, O king, he shall be cast into the den of lions." This accomplished, the presidents and princes thought they had achieved their objective, and that the Hebrew Daniel would soon be thrown to the lions and torn to bits, thus no longer blocking their own crooked endeavors in the kingdom.

According to the law of the Medes and the Persians, a decree once signed *must stand.* It could not be revoked or altered. The presidents and princes therefore knew that the king could not break his word. If all went according to their plan, then the decree which Darius had just signed would mean death to Daniel, for they knew that he would never betray his faith in God nor deny his testimony. They knew him well enough to know that even the threat of death would not change his daily routine in worshipping Jehovah God.

We come now to our text—verse 10 in the passage quoted from Daniel 6:

"Now when Daniel knew that the writing was signed, he went into his house; and his windows being open in his chamber toward Jerusalem, he kneeled upon his knees three times a day, and prayed, and gave thanks before his God, as he did aforetime."

There are six things I want us to notice in this verse concerning Daniel:

1.   He was a man of prayer:

When he learned that the decree was signed—a decree that could mean his death—"he went into his house *and prayed."*

Evidently Daniel's home was his place of refuge. In Daniel 2:17 we learn that after asking the king for time to seek an interpretation of the strange dream, Daniel *"went to his house"* to desire "mercies of the God of heaven concerning this secret." And now, under stress of denying his God or facing death in the lions' den, he again *"went into his house,"* and again he sought fellowship with God.

Undoubtedly the walls of Daniel's home, his place of refuge, afforded a feeling of security that the outside world did not provide — and that should be true of every Christian home. Great Christians make great homes, and great homes make a great church. Daniel's home was a sanctuary when his soul was troubled and when danger threatened. It was there that he communed with God.

I wonder what you or I would have done in like circumstances. Faced with Daniel's problem, would we have *panicked* — or would we have *prayed*? Daniel could have protested to the king, or he could have tried to gain sympathy from his friends in the kingdom. He had a perfect right to demand an audience with the king — after all, he was a member of the king's cabinet.

But this wise Hebrew sought an audience with One much higher than the king of Babylon. He drew near to God in order that God might draw near to him and reveal His will and His plan. We know from the context of this verse that prayer was Daniel's daily practice. He never did anything until he first sought God's advice in prayer. You and I would do well to follow his example.

2. He was a man of great courage:

Daniel went into his house to pray, *"his windows being open."* I do not doubt for one minute that the devil whispered in Daniel's ear, "Don't be foolish! Be sensible. Don't ask for trouble — trouble will come soon enough without your asking for it. Close your windows, close the shutters, and pray in secret! You might prolong your arrest for a little while — you might even escape the decree altogether. At least it seems worth trying."

Yes, I believe Satan whispered temptation to Daniel — and it might have been true that Daniel could have escaped arrest for a little while by praying secretly — but it seems reasonable to suppose that if he had been afraid for his *enemies* to hear his prayer, *GOD might have REFUSED to hear it*!

Jesus commands us, "Fear not them which kill the body, but are not able to kill the soul: but rather fear him (the devil) which is able to destroy both soul and body in hell" (Matt. 10:28). Daniel was in complete agreement with the Psalmist: "The Lord is on my side; I will not fear: What can man do unto me?" (Psalm 118:6).

If we fear our enemies more than we fear God, if our fear of man is stronger than our faith in God, then certainly we have no right to expect Him to hear us when we pray.

If Daniel had closed his windows before he prayed he would most assuredly have ruined his testimony, and I personally believe he would have hindered the effectiveness of his prayer. He did not have Romans 8:31 in print as we have it in the Word of God today, but down in his heart he had the message: "If God be FOR us, who can be against us?" He not only knew a *historical* God, he knew God *personally*. He believed in a God who was near in time of trouble, a very present help—a God who was able to deliver *in spite* of the devil.

3. He was a man of great faith:

Paul lists the heroes of faith in Hebrews 11, and in verse 33 he mentions those "who through faith . . . stopped the mouths of lions." *Daniel* unquestionably stands as one of God's heroes of faith.

117

Daniel went into his house to pray, the windows of his house were open, and he prayed before the window that opened *"toward Jerusalem."* I cannot *prove* that there were other windows in Daniel's house, but common sense assures me that there must have been windows on *all* sides of it. Having won for himself a place of prominence in the Babylonian court, it seems likely that he lived in one of the king's houses. It hardly seems that he would have lived in a hut or a house of poor means. I am sure there were windows opening in more than one direction.

One thing is certain: Daniel's windows were not open simply for the purpose of permitting fresh air and sunshine to enter his room — no indeed! But beyond the distant horizon lay a city—the city of his fathers, the holy city of God, the city of the coming King! And as Daniel looked toward Jerusalem, *faith burned in his soul!*

He remembered the God of Abraham, the God of Isaac and Jacob. Abraham's God was HIS God, the old city of Jerusalem was his real home. He was now a stranger in a strange land, but *some day* his faith in God would be honored and his nation would go home to Jerusalem. That is why he kept his windows open toward the Holy City. A man of such faith as *Daniel* could have prayed in a back room of his house, he could have set up his worship in some curtained, secluded spot away from the light and anything that might distract. But he chose to pray before an open window, with his face toward his beloved city, Jerusalem.

4.   He was a man of great humility:

In his house, before his windows that opened toward Jerusalem, *"he kneeled down upon his knees . . .* and prayed." This man was an outstanding personality. He had been appointed to a place of prominence and authority

118

which, in a lesser person, could easily have made him proud. He could have become arrogant and demanding, as befitted his position in the kingdom; but the power he wielded in Babylon and the exalted place he occupied had not made him proud. As he approached God in prayer, he knelt upon his knees in humble reverence.

It is interesting to note, however, that the *only* time this great man knelt was when he came to God in prayer. He often had occasion to enter into the presence of the king of Babylon. He held audience with the dignitaries of his day. But he knelt before none save his God.

Early in his Babylonian captivity Daniel had "purposed in his heart" that he would not defile himself with the king's wine and meat, and he stayed figuratively at the feet of God — yet his very strength lay in the fact that he humbled himself before God. On his knees, he reached beyond the stars! He recognized the constant presence of God and he honored Him with a humble, contrite heart. A spiritual giant by any standard, Daniel was especially great in his humility.

During my years in the ministry I have witnessed men come to their ruin in spiritual matters because of pride. As long as they were just parishioners in the pew they were humble, consecrated, dedicated Christians; but when given a place of authority—deacon, steward, Sunday school superintendent—it was not long until they began to think of themselves as so important and indispensable that the church could not get along without them!

With God, the way UP is DOWN. Men are at their greatest when they are on their knees in holy submission to Almighty God. Daniel was great in wisdom, he was great in courage, he was great in faith, and in spite of his exalted position in Babylon, he was humble before God.

5. He was great in his persistence:

Persistence goes a long way when praying, and Daniel "kneeled upon his knees *three times a day*, and prayed." Praying was not an intermittent practice with Daniel — it was an established *habit*. He did not use prayer as a fire escape, a life jacket, or an insurance policy. He was not content to simply place his request or need before God and then rest. He continually stormed the throne of heaven. He persisted in his efforts until God heard and something happened. Undoubtedly this accounted for his mighty victories in prayer.

We read of one such experience in Daniel 10:1—13:

"In the third year of Cyrus king of Persia a thing was revealed unto Daniel, whose name was called Belteshazzar; and the thing was true, but the time appointed was long: and he understood the thing, and had understanding of the vision.

"In those days I Daniel was mourning three full weeks. I ate no pleasant bread, neither came flesh nor wine in my mouth, neither did I anoint myself at all, till three whole weeks were fulfilled. And in the four and twentieth day of the first month, as I was by the side of the great river, which is Hiddekel; then I lifted up mine eyes, and looked, and behold a certain man clothed in linen, whose loins were girded with fine gold of Uphaz: His body also was like the beryl, and His face as the appearance of lightning, and His eyes as lamps of fire, and His arms and His feet like in colour to polished brass, and the voice of His words like the voice of a multitude.

"And I Daniel alone saw the vision: for the men that were with me saw not the vision; but a great quaking fell upon them, so that they fled to hide themselves. Therefore I was left alone, and saw this great vision, and there remained no strength in me: for my comeliness was turned in me into corruption, and I retained no strength. Yet heard I the voice of His words: and when I heard the voice of His words, then was I in a deep sleep on my face, and my face toward the ground.

"And, behold, an hand touched me, which set me upon my knees and upon the palms of my hands. And He said unto me, O Daniel, a man greatly beloved, understand the words that I speak unto thee, and stand upright: for unto thee am I now sent. And when He had spoken this word unto me, I stood trembling. Then said He unto me, Fear not, Daniel: for from the first day that thou didst set thine heart to understand, and to chasten thyself before thy God, thy words were heard, and I am come for thy words. But the prince of the kingdom of Persia withstood me one and twenty days: but, lo, Michael, one of the chief princes, came to help me; and I remained there with the kings of Persia."

In these verses we learn that on one occasion Daniel fasted and prayed for three weeks — and if the answer had not come in three weeks, I do not doubt that he would have *continued* to pray until it DID come. Daniel believed in God, he believed in his own mission on earth, he believed that God had put him here for a purpose; therefore he could pray in faith, believing that God would hear and answer.

This is true prayer. With sadness I confess that there is very little real praying in our churches today. Most prayer meetings are little more than social gatherings, and more time is usually spent discussing clothes, weather, church programs, and denominational business than is spent in prayer, pouring out sincere petitions to Almighty God.

Today the liberals and modernists would consider Daniel as fanatical and reckless. He did not pray a little sentence prayer and then say "Amen." He prayed three times a day—morning, noon, and night.

If Daniel were on earth today, and if he should go to the ministerial association for advice, the chairman of the association would probably say, "Brother Daniel, since

121

the decree has been made and signed, if you *must* pray, go into your house and close the door. Better still, *go into the closet* — and once a day will be often enough to pray. After all, God knows your heart, He knows the predicament you are in, and there is no reason why you should jeopardize your very life by praying where you can be seen, or by praying three times a day."

Had someone given Daniel that kind of advice, he would have paid no attention to it. He could reach beyond the king's decree; *he knew the King of kings!* And as was his custom, when prayer time came he went into his house, knelt before the windows that were opened toward the Holy City—and kneeling before God *he prayed* — and the demons in hell must have trembled as the petitions of that mighty prayer warrior bombarded the gates of heaven! Daniel prayed in faith, and he prayed persistently.

6. He prayed with thanksgiving:

". . . He prayed and *gave thanks* before his God, as he did aforetime." There is something strange about this. It is easy to praise and thank God when something good has come our way, when some great burden has been lifted, or when a great deliverance has already come; but beloved, *Daniel praised and thanked God BEFORE deliverance came!*

The decree had been signed and sealed with the seal of the Medes and the Persians—a seal that could not be broken. Once given, the king's decree was *absolute* and unalterable. Daniel knew that if he made request of any other save King Darius, he faced the den of lions. The threat of death hung over his head — and yet, facing these facts, he prayed—*and then gave thanks to God for the answer he knew would come!*

Daniel knew that the ways of God are beyond our

122

understanding, and are sometimes unpredictable. Certainly he *hoped* that God would intervene and save him from the fate that threatened him; but if it would be more to God's glory for him to be *thrown into* the den of lions, he could still pray "Thy will be done," and give thanks for God's will in his life.

Daniel's attitude here was the same as that of Shadrach, Meshach, and Abednego when Nebuchadnezzar had demanded that they worship the image he had set up. They refused—and Nebuchadnezzar said, "Ye shall be cast the same hour into the midst of a burning fiery furnace; *and who is that God that shall deliver you out of my hands?*"

The three young Hebrews replied, "O Nebuchadnezzar, we are not careful to answer thee in this matter. *If it be so, our God whom we serve IS ABLE* to deliver us from the burning fiery furnace, and He WILL deliver us out of thine hand, O king. BUT IF NOT, BE IT KNOWN UNTO THEE, O KING, THAT WE WILL NOT SERVE THY GODS, NOR WORSHIP THE GOLDEN IMAGE WHICH THOU HAST SET UP" (Dan. 3:15–18).

By his actions, Daniel said to his enemies, "My God CAN deliver me, He is ABLE to deliver me, He WILL deliver me if it is to my good and to His glory. But if He does NOT see fit to deliver me from the lions' den, then be it known to one and all that I will kneel upon my knees before my open window, facing toward our Holy City, and I will pray three times daily just as I did before the decree was given!"

Daniel could have panicked — but instead, *he prayed and gave thanks.* He undoubtedly prayed for God's will in deliverance from the king's decree, and I personally believe that he *gave thanks* for past experiences and past mercies. When the Hebrews were taken captive by Babylon, we learn that Daniel, Shadrach, Meshach, and Abednego were picked from a group and placed in the king's court to be taught the learning and the tongue of the Chaldeans:

"And the king appointed them a daily provision of the king's meat, and of the wine which he drank: so nourishing them three years, that at the end thereof they might stand before the king. . . *But Daniel purposed in his heart that he would not defile himself* with the portion of the king's meat, nor with the wine which he drank: therefore he requested of the prince of the eunuchs that he might not defile himself. . . Then said Daniel . . . Prove thy servants, I beseech thee, ten days; and let them give us pulse to eat, and water to drink. Then let our countenances be looked upon before thee, and the countenance of the children that eat of the portion of the king's meat: and as thou seest, deal with thy servants. So he consented to them in this matter, and proved them ten days. And at the end of ten days their countenances appeared fairer and fatter in flesh than all the children which did eat the portion of the king's meat. . . And in all matters of wisdom and understanding, that the king enquired of them, he found them ten times better than all the magicians and astrologers that were in all his realm. And Daniel continued even unto the first year of king Cyrus" (Dan. 1:3–21).

The day that Daniel purposed in his heart that he would not defile himself was the day that marked the beginning of his greatness, and I believe his prayer of thanksgiving included praise and thanks to God for that experience.

I also believe he thanked God for the settled peace he had in his heart, even though he faced possible death in the lions' den! Daniel was familiar with the power of the Medes and the Persians, he fully recognized the danger he faced at their hands if he disobeyed the king's decree; but even in the face of that danger he had perfect peace of mind and heart—the peace of God "that passeth all understanding."

124

I am sure you are familiar with the rest of the story—how Daniel's enemies gathered outside his house and found him praying; how they reported this to King Darius, and how the king, displeased with himself for having *made* such a decree in the first place (certainly he had intended no harm to Daniel), tried "till the going down of the sun" to find some way to break the decree and save Daniel. But the presidents and princes reminded him, "Know, O king, that the law of the Medes and Persians is, *That no decree nor statute which the king establisheth may be changed.*"

So the king commanded Daniel to be cast into the den of lions — but listen to the testimony of Darius as he spoke to Daniel: *"Thy God whom thou servest continually, He will deliver thee!"* What a testimony! What a life Daniel must have lived before that heathen king!

It is entirely possible that Daniel had one of the best night's rest of his entire life that night. The angel of God closed the mouths of the lions, the heat from their bodies warmed the pit where they were confined, and Daniel spent the hours in perfect peace.

It was quite another story with King Darius: "The king went to his palace, and passed the night fasting: neither were instruments of musick brought before him: and his sleep went from him" (Dan. 6:18).

The circumstances that could have meant his destruction became a steppingstone to greater things for Daniel—the man of God who prayed when he might have panicked.

If I could have but one wish, if God would grant me such, I would wish that I could be as Daniel was . . . I wish I might have the wisdom and the courage he displayed, the faith he exercised, the humility he demonstrated, the persistence and perseverance in prayer that he had — and

125

I wish I could be as thankful to God for my blessings as Daniel was for his!

To you young Christians who may be reading these lines—if you are truly born again and you feel that God has called you to serve Him, do what *Daniel* did in the very beginning of his Babylonian captivity: *Purpose in your heart* that you will not defile yourself with the things of this world.

His Word promises, "Trust in the Lord with all thine heart; and lean not unto thine own understanding. *In all thy ways acknowledge Him, and He shall direct thy paths*" (Prov. 3:5,6).

Purpose in your heart, here and now, that you will fear God ONLY, obey God SUPREMELY, and "whether therefore ye eat, or drink, or whatsoever ye do, do all to the glory of God" (I Cor. 10:31). *Dare to be a Daniel!*